# Michael S. Piazza

## Sexuality & Christianity

# Our Tribe

## Queer Folks, God, Jesus and the Bible

# Our Tribe

## Queer Folks, God, Jesus and the Bible

### Millennium Edition
### Updated and Revised

**Rev. Nancy Wilson**

ALAMO SQUARE PRESS
New Mexico

Library of Congress Catalog Card Number: 95-12266

ISBN: 1-886360-10-3

10   9   8   7   6   5   4   3   2   1

4

**To Paula, for a wonderful life of love and surprises.**

**and for listening to all my stories...**

*Set me as a seal upon your heart,*
*as a seal upon your arm;*
*for love is strong as death,*
*passion as fierce as the grave.*
*It's flashes are flashes of fire,*
*a raging flame.*
*Many waters cannot quench love,*
*neither can floods drown it.*
*If one offered love*
*all the wealth of her house*
*it would be utterly scorned.*

Song of Solomon 8:6 and 7

# Table of Contents

# Preface

In 1995, the first edition of *Our Tribe* by Rev. Nancy Wilson was published by HarperSan Francisco and very well received. It was a longer book, including Nancy's warm, moving stories along with her expansive vision of Bible interpretation. The book sold out quickly. However HarperSan Francisco, dealing with shifting priorities, allowed it to go out of print.

Since Nancy originally wrote the book, her rich collection of stories about being an out lesbian minister, and a gay representative in the Christian ecumenical movement have continued to accumulate, while fine definitive works on gay-friendly interpretations of the Bible have become more available.

In this Millennium Edition, Nancy updates and elaborates on her wonderful adventures. Meanwhile she works diligently preparing an additional volume of *Outing the Bible* for later publication.

Bert Herrman,
Editor & Publisher

# Acknowledgments

In some ways, writing a book is a very solitary thing. In many other ways, though, if you are the pastor of a church, it is not! This book originated in the context of pastoring MCC Los Angeles.

Through moving many times, earthquakes, mortgage woes, and untold grief and loss, and the rough and tumble of being a church in the heart of the gay and lesbian community, I have learned from the members, friends, staff and board of MCC Los Angeles the truth of Psalm 46:

> *God is our refuge and strength,*
> *a very present help in trouble.*
> *Therefore we will not fear, though*
> *the earth should change,*
> *though the mountains shake in the*
> *heart of the sea*

Thanks to the wonderful pastoral staff and board of MCC Los Angeles, who continue to inspire me, and to provide support, not only for pastoring MCC Los Angeles, but for endeavors such as this.

Thanks to the many other MCC Los Angeles members and friends who have taught me so much.

Special thanks to those who assisted in the making of this book: Bless you, Sandy Williams for trips to the library, and Jakely of Forman Graphics, Norm Mason, Rev. Evelyn Kinser.

Thanks to Bert Herrman for taking a chance on editing and reprinting *Out Tribe*.

This book would not have happened without Fr. Malcolm Boyd. When we were doing a "gig" together in San Francisco, Malcolm told me I had to write this book. You are my fairy godfather!

Thank you, Rev. Troy Perry, for starting MCC; for seeing my potential in those early days; for being an incredibly openhearted, open-minded leader; for being willing to be the prophet of God.

I want to remember some of my heavenly friends, in addition to the ones who come up in the stories that follow: Vicki Goldish, I still miss you; Rev. Sandy Taylor; Rev. Jim Harris; Dr. Gary McClelland; Edith Perry; Rev. Carlos Jones, Kath Staples and hundreds of others. Dr. John Boswell, whose brilliance can never be replaced, what a model of courageous gay scholarship! Thank you Rev. Danny Mahoney, assistant pastor extraordinaire, who on your deathbed told me to finish the book. Thanks to Patrick, who stuck around only long enough to take care of Danny.

Thank you God, finally, for my lover and spouse Paula, to whom this book is dedicated, my mother Barbara, brothers David and Mark, and for my dear father Ralph, whose laughter, love and playfulness are such a blessed memory.

# Introduction—Tribal Tales

Theologically speaking, I'm trying on the label *queer millennialist*. No one knows what that is, and we're all bored by and sick of most theological labels and categories. Many of these labels are breaking down anyway, as enormous cultural changes take place. Also, "queer millennialist" sounds both playful and radical.

I'll start by telling a sweet queer story. In addition to being the pastor of the oldest publicly queer church in America (and perhaps the world), I have been, since 1976, Metropolitan Community Church's (MCC's) official lesbian ecu-terrorist. (Actual title: "Chief Ecumenical Officer.") It has been my job until recently to coordinate the strategies and policies of our Ecumenical Witness and Ministry Department. I still occasionally work with and train MCC clergy and laity to interact with (that is, terrorize) ecumenical (interreligious) organizations.[1] This is, of course, nonviolent terrorism. I realize that "terrorism" is a loaded word these days. However, I use it because we queer folk have literally been terrorized by a homophobic world, and seem to emotionally terrorize ecumenical organizations just by showing up.

When the World Council of Churches came to Los Angeles after the uprising of April 29, 1992, I was called upon to participate with others in "sharing our perspectives" about life in L.A. vis-à-vis the various police departments, conditions for our community and other issues.

The Council decided to host listening posts in the African American, Korean-American, Hispanic-American, and other communities; the gay and lesbian community was a last-minute add-on. Seeing the lineup of speakers, I knew it was my job to get more representation from gay and lesbian people of color in particular. But I knew something else was also missing. We ecu-terrorists tend to be rather "churchy" folks, able to speak fluently the language of the "religion." What would it be like for the World Council of Churches to hear just raw, queer rage, unecumenized, uncensored?

Plus, as a meddling pastor type, I knew that people like Rob needed to be heard by just such a group. A few months before, after a community meeting, Rob and I went to a popular new gay coffee shop in West Hollywood. We had been working on a project together: the third monument in the world to honor gay and lesbian protest. It was to memorialize several actions that had taken place on the Crescent Heights Triangle in West Hollywood, the most recent of which was the beginning of two solid weeks of nonviolent protests against Governor Pete Wilson's vetoing of the gay and lesbian rights bill, AB101. (In 1999, this Triangle would be named for the martyred Matthew Shephard). Sitting in that coffee shop, Rob had finally popped *the* question: "How can you be a Christian? You seem like a really great person." Rob was a 30ish, wide-eyed activist still struggling with addiction recovery issues and in love with queer politics (most of the time). He was a very tall, handsome, fair-haired, beach-boy type who still had traces of adolescent gangliness.

I tried to account for myself. I tried not to be defensive about the Church's wretched record of sexism, racism and homophobia. To say a few good words about Jesus. And then without having said too much, to turn the tables (I have always liked *this* part of following Jesus.). So I said, "Did you grow up in church?"

Rob flushed. Then he grinned, "Yeah, I grew up going to Lutheran parochial school."

"So," I said, "when did it happen? When did they break your heart?" Bingo. He had that "How did you know?" look on his face. I find that for many gay and lesbian people, "it" (having your heart broken by the church) happened long before they knew they were queer. "Oh, yeah," Rob said, "there was the Jack Benny thing."

The Jack Benny thing. At six, Rob had taken piano lessons from a Lutheran church schoolteacher. While on his way to his piano lesson one day, he heard the news that Jack Benny had just died. Rob loved Jack Benny. I immediately understood. As a child, I had loved the comics and impersonators the best. There was Jack Benny, effeminate violin player, making fun of himself for our enjoyment. People admired and loved Jack Benny, and as queer as it may sound, he made Rob feel safer in the world. I know he made me feel safer, too. Full of grief and questions, Rob asked

**14**

his piano teacher, "Will Jack Benny go to heaven?"

"No," came the clear-cut answer. No. No. He was not Christian, or Lutheran, or *something*. So Rob learned that God didn't love Jack Benny. Or at least that Lutherans didn't believe that God loved Jack Benny. Rob's heart asked, How can I love someone or something that God doesn't love enough to take into heaven? Or that God even hates? Everything shattered in Rob's very tender and new life of faith. And it never got put back together again, at least not in the Church.

Incomprehensible cruelty: heaven without Jack Benny. Without comedy or effeminate men. Who wants to go there? An exclusive, hard nosed God, the God who made Jack Benny, who could with his eyes, the flick of a wrist, the perfect timing, make the world laugh! That same God wouldn't take Jack in? *What's wrong with this picture?* Just telling the story was painful for Rob. At first he thought it was silly. But then it became clear. *The Jack Benny thing* was Rob's first clue that the church that had raised him taught of a God who might not really love him after all. If God didn't want Jack Benny, what chance would Rob have? And how could he appeal this decision? So Rob left the Lutherans to their Jack Benny-less heaven.

I told Rob that it was just possible that what he had really rejected was not God and maybe not even Christianity but a very tragic interpretation of both. I saw the spark of hope in Rob's eyes. It was that spark, the hope that survives shame and rage, that I wanted the World Council folks to see. And they did. Just months after our coffeehouse encounter, Rob testified before members of the Central Committee of the World Council of Churches about gay and lesbian oppression and about his struggle with this "God thing." So the conversation had appropriately shifted from Jack Benny to God. Rob addressed the Central Committee as a queer national and was eloquent and passionate.

Rob ducked in and out of church at MCC for the next two years, full of queer ambivalence. Before he died of AIDS, he called me from his hospital bed with a great sermon idea for me about somebody he remembered from his Lutheran Sunday school days. Some guy named Job. "I think Job was refusing to be a victim! Like me—why don't you preach about that?"

15

## Millennial Musings

As we begin the third millennium, we have closed the books on what politicians, sociologists, historians, theologians, and others are calling the most violent century in the recorded history of the world. (By the way, it was reported after the Jeffrey Dahmer tragedy that a disproportionate number of mass murderers are *Lutherans*. This may be little comfort to most of us, but Rob frankly felt a little validated by that troubling statistic.) Perhaps living in Los Angeles recently has made me view the state of the world with special intensity. In Los Angeles, the First and Third Worlds are meeting more and more. Los Angeles is a city teeming with languages and cultures in a shifting human landscape. Neighborhoods change as fast as do the stores in minimalls.

It is also a city located in a desert. This means that the land itself is really only created to handle a sparse density of life, especially human life. The millions who inhabit this region do so unnaturally, as a result of human manipulation, technology and intervention. When the very natural (for the most part) phenomena of earthquake, fire and floods occur, the toll of life and property is astronomically exaggerated by the population explosion of the last half of the 20th century.

In the first years of the last decade of the second millennium, in Los Angeles, we had frightening, apocalyptic experiences: devastating fires, prolonged recession, political uprisings, the worst flooding in 500 years in the region, and a devastating earthquake. Is Los Angeles a symbol of the last dying cry of the violent 20th century, or a peek into what is to come?

I don't know if anyone has managed to capture the effect this has had on the people who continue to live here. Somehow all the sunny promise of California as the land of prosperity and fun and Hollywood glitz (the American version of the Promised Land) has literally crashed and burned. We can't quite count on it like we did. Human need and human greed have collided here in a millennial drama.

My use of the word millennial is both serious and playful. Millennialist thought in Judaism and Christianity is a particular form of eschatology (that is, thinking about the end times—how the world will end, how God will wrap it all up). The actual word millennium comes from the root "mil," which means thousand, as in "thousand years." In Jewish and Christian writings there is the promise of an *interregnum*—in-between time that may last literally for one thousand years or for some symbolic amount of time. Rabbis, church fathers, church reformers and 19th- and 20th-century American religious sectarian leaders have debated for over two millennia about the details. There are those Christians who believe it will happen before Christ returns or the Messiah comes; others believe it will happen after Christ returns. And, of course, there are many whose cultures and calendars didn't count this as a millennium shift at all, but, who, nevertheless have been dragged into all the fuss by global Christian economic hegemony.

Sometimes this imagined Millennial time period is called the "eighth day of creation." According to some, it will be characterized by any number of things: the destruction of evil, the creation of a new heaven and earth, and the enjoyment on earth of eternal bliss. Some prophets predict the return of the *ten lost tribes*, while others describe it as the gathering together of *people and tribes*. Millennial fantasies have included predictions of unprecedented earthly fertility, peace, and harmony not only among humans but among animals and between animals and humans. Some have imagined endless sumptuous dining and even uninterrupted enjoyment of nuptial bliss!

Millennial thought has often been overtly material and sensuous. But there is also a downside to the millennial vision: a prediction of Armageddon, the world rule of the anti-Christ, suffering, wars and rumors of wars. And, of course, there are debates about whether such suffering will follow or precede an idyllic millennium.

Narrow, literal views of the millennium have characterized some of the more bizarre cults and some particularly negative, exclusionary Protestant sects. Is fascination with millennialism always tied to the more neurotic, escapist forms of faith? On the other hand, a lot of the proliferating New Age philosophies and theologies also abound with quasi-millennialist visions.

When I use the word millennialist, I am not choosing among several traditional, fixed views of the "end times." I simply want to understand the human longing for "heaven on earth"; the persistence of the vision of the "peaceable kingdom" in the midst of contemporary planetary crisis; and a little bit of what Jesus meant by this "kingdom" that is in our midst and yet to come.

According to some of us, the world's calendar has turned the page on one millennium and open the page to another. On the eve of that millennial shift, the gay and lesbian movement has appeared. Judy Grahn offers a wonderful metaphor for this gay and lesbian millennial surge:

> Purple book jackets appeared on books and dictionaries produced by gay poets and writers of both sexes, and purple T-shirts announced gay slogans of affirmation from diverse groups of people from all over the country. As though some mysterious hand had planted bulbs all over the land, we lavender folk sprang up spontaneously flowering in the color we had learned as an identifying mark of our culture when it was subterranean and a secret.[2]

What about the possibility of a queer millennium? Rev. Troy Perry and other the community called for a "Millennial March on Washington" for the year 2000 that has provoked even more than the usual political squabbling in the Gay/Lesbian/Bisexual/Transgendered communities. Are marches on Washington old hat? Does it matter if such a march affects Washington at all? Is the purpose of the march really to inspire a new generation of activists, or to have a big party, or a fund-raising venture for capital hungry national organizations? You can listen all day to the detractors and cynics. But I do think there is within our communities a longing for a new "new day" that, in some hard to put your finger on way, the millennium inspires.

Does it sound too greedy? A queer millennium? A queer interregnum, a truly in-between time. A *time-out* for the planet! After all, we queer folks are the quintessential in-between folks. Judy Grahn, Mark Thompson, and many others have been documenting the "in-between" gay and lesbian culture and sensibility for decades.

So just what in the world is going on? I think we are having a violent reaction of rage and helplessness because of the destabilization of nations and economies, overpopulation and the resulting poverty and hunger, and the sweeping technological changes that do not seem to solve these problems but only simultaneously to worsen them and to make us more acutely aware of them on a daily basis. There is much debate about whether or not we are simply polluting and poisoning ourselves to death. Some say the environmentalists are a bunch of fanatics who don't appreciate the resiliency of nature. But the truth seems to be that there is a planetary immunological crisis going on, born of the increasing toxicity of the environment—a universal AIDS.

In such a toxic environment, the poor, the minorities and the politically vulnerable populations will be the first to exhibit signs and symptoms of the deteriorating immunological picture. It is the canary-in-the-mines syndrome. When miners wanted to know if a particular mine shaft was safe from poison gases, they sent in a canary first. If the canary returned, the miners felt safe to go in. On our planet today, poor people, people of color, women and children, and gays and lesbians are the canaries (or sitting ducks, if you prefer). Those who have any kind of privilege (gender, race, class, sexuality, age) are better able, for a time, to buffer and insulate themselves from the toxic environment from AIDS, cancer and other diseases. But not forever.

There is also an increasing moral and religious toxicity in reaction to so much social upheaval, change and worldwide political challenges. This phenomenon is called in many religions fundamentalism. In a time of increasing relativity of values, morality and religion, fundamentalism provides absolutes and identifies the enemies. It is a kind of collective mental illness that includes obsessive thinking, tunnel vision, and functions much like other addictions. The growing threat of the religious right is being unmasked in our time—that is, in what has popularly been called *the age of rage.*

The last decade or so of the 20th century saw the brutal death, really lynching of Matthew Shepherd, the murders of James Byrd, Billy Jack Gaither, other gay and lesbian people, attacks on transgendered people, people of color, Jews, with increasing viciousness and frequency. Suddenly, we were talking a lot more about hate crimes. Hate crimes directed at those who are perceived as "different" or unwelcome.

### Who are the Gay and Lesbian People?

What does it mean to be a gay or lesbian or bisexual person in this age of rage? It was the poet Judy Grahn who first spoke powerfully to me about an anthropology or sociology of what she calls "transpeople" (a broad category including gay men, lesbians, transvestites and transsexuals). For a long time I have believed that *theological anthropology* (in the old days, this was called the "doctrine of man") was the Church's major problem in acceptance of gays and lesbians. Are gay men and lesbians a *lobby* for a certain kind of behavior that we want the Church to legitimize, or are we a *kind of people?*

19

And if we are a kind of people, just what kind are we? Michael Cartwright[3] has traced the ways African-American writers, historians, sociologists, and theologians have struggled, for centuries with questions about black identity. They had to overcome the poisonous pedagogy of the white Christian slaveholders who exegeted Genesis 9:20-27 and 10:6-11, the story of Ham, in a racist way. Blacks also had to ask the question, "For what reason did God create us? Why did God deliver us from slavery?" Underneath was the question "And why didn't God do it sooner?" or "Why did God let slavery happen at all?"

As a pastor of a multicultural church in Los Angeles, I recall the painful voice on the other end of the phone of a black gay man telling me that his lover, HIV positive and addicted to drugs, had spent the better part of the morning crying out, "Why does God hate us?" He did not mean gay people, or people with AIDS. He meant African-Americans, that particular "us." Does our racial or sexual identity have purpose...meaning? Does our collective suffering or redemption mean anything?

It is relatively new for gays and lesbians to have this question be above ground. The "love that dare not speak its name" did not dare to theologize much about itself, or even to philosophize much, until recent decades. We are new at asking such questions even semipublicly.

The problem with religions that personalize God (like Christianity) is that it then seems illogical not to personalize disaster or triumph. In theological circles, this problem is called theodicy: understanding how evil and oppression can exist in a world created by a good God. As a lesbian pastor in the gay and lesbian community, I have had hundreds of conversations with people agonizing about whether God truly created us as we are. And if so, could God love us; and if so, why was there so much suffering, pain and homophobia?

The truth is, I'm not sure I ever really stopped long enough in the early frenetic, even dangerous days to ask those questions myself. I do, however, remember asking them one night in a restaurant in Vancouver, British Columbia. ("Why does the Church hate us? Where does homophobia come from?")

The occasion was a "top-secret" meeting between the leaders of the National Council of Churches of Christ (NCC) in the United States and the Universal Fellowship of Metropolitan Community Churches (UFMCC) in the summer of 1983.[4] Tensions within the NCC had been

20

mounting over the issue of UFMCC's application for membership. The Eastern Orthodox churches had issued a statement to the press in the spring, indicating that if UFMCC were ever declared eligible for membership by the governing board, they would leave the council. But in fact, the membership committee of the council (which included an Orthodox member) had unanimously voted in March 1982 that we met all five criteria for membership, and a vote by the council to ratify that judgment had already been postponed for a year and a half.

Meanwhile, UFMCC and most of the council were unaware that the president, Bishop James Armstrong, was experiencing a deep emotional crisis that would result in his surprise resignation, surrounded by scandal and rumor, in November 1983. These were the early Reagan years. Ronald Reagan and his administration had no use for the NCC and its liberal reputation. In fact, it was on the heels of the Reagan election that both *Reader's Digest* and *60 Minutes* did very biased and damaging exposes on the political activities of the NCC and the World Council of Churches (WCC). This exposure was a major source of political and financial anxiety for the council. So it was with some dismay that the leadership of the NCC also found itself having to deal with an application for membership from a controversial denomination serving a less-than acceptable minority: homosexuals!

I had admired James Armstrong since my college antiwar activism days. He had *been there*. He was well known for having negotiated with the American Indian Movement (AIM) in the early '70s during the siege at Wounded Knee. He was a classic liberal-activist churchman. I knew gay people who knew him and had worked for him. When he had treated MCC so very coolly in the early days of our application process, I felt disappointed. He knew better, I thought. Where was the courageous moral leadership that we needed at this time?

So when a leader of a major U.S. denomination, Dr. Arie Brower, (who later became the General Secretary of the National Council of Churches) called me at my home one late spring morning, proposing a top-level, hush-hush meeting with Rev. Troy Perry and myself, I was open and enthusiastic. At last, a chance to talk face-to-face with Armstrong, Dr. Claire Randall (General Secretary of the NCC and an extraordinary churchwoman), and the leaders of four of the most powerful and traditionally more liberal denominations.

Meanwhile, all was not well at our headquarters in Los Angeles. At the time, I worked full time for the Fellowship as Clerk of the Board of Elders. In late May we had learned of the tragic, mysterious death of Reverend Perry's lover, Greg Cutts. Greg was in the process of emigrating from Canada, after a two-year struggle. Life had been very stressful for Troy and Greg as they tried to manage a long-distance relationship. Both of them were very happy about Greg's impending move. But over the Victoria Day weekend in Canada, Greg died in his sleep. In the chaotic weeks that followed, I informed the NCC of Greg's death and told them that we would have to postpone our meeting.

As it happened, all of them would be in Vancouver in July 1983 for the WCC General Assembly. Our UFMCC finances at the time were strained to the max. But NCC leaders managed to arrange funding for airfare for one of us to Vancouver, and Troy and I went to meet them "off campus" in a nearby restaurant.

I was very worried about Troy and wondered whether or not he should even go to this meeting. But Armstrong had initially talked to him about it—and Troy was curious, I think. To make things more complicated, Greg had died in Vancouver. When we attended the meeting in July, it had only been one month since Troy had been there for Greg's funeral.

We were very cordially greeted in the restaurant. After some small talk, Dr. Brower of the Reformed Church in America, said softly to Troy, "We are sorry to hear about your recent loss." The Hallmark greeting-card phrasing seemed awkward but well-intentioned. And I was grateful that someone had been willing to acknowledge publicly that Troy's lover had died.

What happened then was a classic case study of the relationship of Metropolitan Community Churches to the NCC. Troy misunderstood the offer of condolences. What he did not know is that people in the liberal middle-class world of ecumenical politics and etiquette say things like that to put to *rest* a certain matter, not to open it up. The people in that room, though they had known each other for years, knew little, if anything, about each other's personal lives. That became all too evident when Armstrong later resigned. But Troy mistakenly thought he was in a safe place—in the company of Christian leadership in the U.S. People who, like him, knew the loneliness and pressures of leading a denomination—people who loved the Lord. So when someone reached out with condolences, Troy just opened up. He told them about Greg's death. About how hard it was to meet his spouse's parents for the first time at his funeral. He cried. He spoke very simply and sweetly about his love for Greg and about how he met Greg. All the time I watched their faces. How much they did not want to be hearing this! How unaccustomed they were to this level of intimate, open, vulnerable sharing of love and grief. He pressed every homophobic, classist, sex-phobic, intimacy-phobic button they had. They looked stunned and helpless, shifting in their seats. They impatiently cleared their throats. I, too, felt helpless. I was certain that if one of them said anything to hurt him, I'd simply have to turn some tables over right there in the restaurant. Mercifully, Troy stopped. We took a breath, and Bishop Armstrong switched the subject and got down to it.

What I did not know was that not everyone at that table knew what he was about to say. Bishop Armstrong leaned toward us, looked right at me, and said (I'm paraphrasing, but not too much), "I know you love Jesus Christ and the Church of Jesus Christ. If you really do, you will spare us the agony of having to take a divisive vote in the fall that will only cause you pain. Please prayerfully consider withdrawing your application for membership." I don't remember if I even looked at Troy, although I swear I could feel his blood run cold. But Armstrong had addressed me. In a flash, I pictured the dear faces of my UFMCC colleagues and friends as I would try to explain to them how withdrawing our application was the right thing to do, what Jesus really wanted. Then, thankfully, my crap detector kicked in.

Somehow I managed not to throw up the expensive salmon dinner and to reply. Basically, I said, "No way." And something like "And don't think that by withdrawing our application it will spare us pain. Gay and lesbian people experience pain at the hands of the Church of Jesus Christ every day. We are prepared to endure the pain of rejection as our cross to bear at this time in history. One of the reasons MCC is coming to the NCC is to witness visibly to the spiritual awakening in the gay and lesbian community and also to make visible the lethal homophobia of the Church. We're sorry, but we think Jesus is with us in this process, and if you do the right thing, God will be with the NCC."

That ended the discussion. Afterward Troy let me know that he would leave the ecu-politics to me; he preferred the cutthroat secular politicians any day. But to the point of the story: sometime during that evening I managed to spend a little time with Claire Randall. I told her about MCC's worldwide ministry, including our predominantly heterosexual churches in Nigeria among the "untouchable" people. Suddenly she became interested. I enjoyed her questions, her interest in UFMCC, her insights, and what felt like her genuine respect and support of a kind. And then I asked the question. I had never personally asked this question of anyone. I chose this strange moment to ask my question of this older, never married, close-to-retirement feminist veteran of countless ecumenical skirmishes and adventures. I remember that very private moment when I simply asked her, "Why do you think there is so much fear and resistance toward UFMCC?" (Really: Why do they hate us so?) She sighed, looked nowhere particular, and said, "Well, I guess when you talk about sex and the Bible in the same breath, they just go nuts."

Not an explanation but an excellent description: "They just go nuts."

A few months into my co-pastorate at MCC Boston in 1973, I was consecrating communion. It was a warm summer evening. Suddenly, from the second pew, a man none of us had seen before got up, ran to the front of the sanctuary, knocked over the communion elements, punched me in the face, and ran out of the church before anyone could stop him.

They just go nuts.

## So, Who are We?

Who are gay men and lesbians? Sometimes, in my deepest self, I feel like we are some ancient tribal remnant that has survived and that now appears to be dispersed among every other earthly tribe—a transtribal tribe!

But others see homosexuality as purely a social construct, with no visible, demonstrable core or essence. A kind of behavior(s) so despised that those who practice it seek to take refuge in the concept of homosexuality as an identity.

Then there's all the hypothalamus hype: genetics, brain components. Next they'll be feeling the bumps on our skulls. Still others see homosexuality as a matrix of factors, causes, constructions. The truth is, I don't know what to think. Nor do many lesbians and gay men. Some of us do believe that we chose our orientation. Most, in my experience, speak of it more in terms of a discovery—a gift given before we were aware of receiving it.

Over the years I have had several experiences of what I feel is something akin to lesbian and gay tribal memory. I say this with a sense of caution and humility. For me, being a lesbian was not a choice. The only choice was how I would or would not accept who I was. And it was not only a discovery. For me—and this is admittedly romantic—it has also felt like my destiny. Martin Buber said, "We must believe in Destiny, and that it stands in need of us."[5]

In June of 1972 I marched down Fifth Avenue with my lesbian friend Jean Gralley in one of New York's earliest Gay Pride parades. I'd only been out of the closet for three months. And there I was walking down Fifth Avenue next to Jill Johnston, author of *Lesbian Nation*, columnist for the *Village Voice*, ( the original "queer national"), and author Isabel Miller. I don't think I ever closed my mouth for four hours. The most queers I'd ever seen in one place together before that had been maybe five or six. We were at least 50,000 people: drag queens, leather queens, lesbian separatists: a raucous, irreverent, heart-pounding throng. We marched breathing fire and freedom. I learned a new word that day: "dyke." It made me smile when I said it, though I couldn't tell you why. As we moved up Fifth Avenue, I fell in love with this movement. Whatever part of me was still doubting, still wondering if I was not just in love with this one particular woman—just a phase, a fluke—evaporated in the steamy June New York Sunday after noon heat. Everyone smiled at everyone, we delighted in one another, no strangers among us: my tribal initiation.

It also became my big parental coming out day. After a long, full day at gay pride, during which Jean invited me to my first MCC service (I refused, thinking it was a silly idea), I took the train and a cab home to my parent's house on Long Island. My mother was waiting up for me. She had what my brothers and I called "the look." It seems that Barbara Gittings, noted lesbian activist, had been on the *David Suskind show*, and, oops, I had a letter from Barbara sitting in the mail basket by the front door. That, and the fact that she and my father both suspected something during my college graduation, when I couldn't cover up how torn up I was in leaving school. It was apparently quite transparent that I was not torn up about leaving school, but about leaving my first lover, who would be rejoining me in Boston in the fall. I was in love for the first time, and, having been in love themselves, they could see it, even though I struggled and suffered to cover up my joy and grief.

So, this little bit of extra proof, à la Barbara Gittings, was all my mother needed. She confronted me as soon as I walked in the door that hot, June night, that suddenly got a lot hotter for me. It turned all of our lives upside down for many years. It was perhaps the second bravest things I'd done in my life, to answer my mother truthfully when she asked me if Gerry and I were lovers. I was the eldest child after all, responsible, never in trouble in my life. I wanted to vomit, to disappear. I don't think I ever wanted to lie so much in my whole life. After all, I'd lied about much less important things, on occasion. And, I almost did that night.

But, part of me already knew it was futile, or inevitable. I just couldn't betray that first complete love of my life. When I thought of her, which was often, I could not betray the gift of her love, I could not deny that joy. That I had actually had the guts to leap over my own homophobic wall, and make love with a woman I cared deeply about was such an amazing act of courage, the first truly brave (and highly disobedient) thing I had ever done. It was too late to take it back, to shove it in a closet, or bury it in a grave of shame or lies. I was terrified, but I was also glad. The only barrier to being completely out of the closet was my fear of hurting my family and becoming alienated from them. Having crossed that barrier for good, I was free. Excited, terrified and free.

Twenty-three years later, in 1994, the year after my father died, my mother, Jean (who took me to my first Gay Pride parade) and I walked hand in hand down Second Avenue in New York City at the head of the UFMCC contingent in the "Stonewall 25" celebration. A few years before, my Mom and Dad snuck out of church early and attended, in support, the very first Gay Pride parade on Long Island. But never in a million years could I have ever predicted this. My Mom and Jean and I all over CBS, on national news. At one point, my mother and I looked up to see a helicopter flying above us. My Dad loved and serviced helicopters as a mechanic all of his adult life. We smiled , feeling his presence with us.

My mother and I were simply not the same people we had been 23 years before. We had both mellowed, grown, and long since forgiven ourselves and each other. I was so proud of her, and proud to be leading the MCC contingent (Troy was in the front of the parade with the early founders of Gay Liberation), amazed at what can happen to people who keep their hearts and minds open long enough.

I first attended a National Council of Churches Governing Board meeting in May 1982, ten years after my first Gay Pride parade. Adam DeBaugh, a lay leader in UFMCC, and I arrived in Nashville, each of us with some prior ecumenical experience but not with the NCC Governing Board. Almost 300 people met, including the press and visitors, at a large Methodist church in Nashville. We walked in just as the opening service began. All eyes discreetly turned in our direction in a silent, dread-filled chorus of "They're here!" No one officially greeted us, and we hadn't a clue about what to do or whom to talk to.

Later that day a kindly Methodist (Rev. Jeanne Audrey Powers, who would later come out as a lesbian), asked me in hushed tones, "Well, what is your strategy?" I remember feeling totally naked ("Strategy! Oh, no! I forgot to wear my strategy!"), like one of those nightmares where you show up to teach or preach without your sermon notes...or clothing ...or something essential. We had a kind of ecumenical innocence. We had applied for membership and assumed we'd just go through their process. Why did we need a strategy? So, strategically naked, after the opening worship service, we positioned ourselves quite awkwardly, as if we were ushers or greeters, and shook hands and handed out pamphlets (like church bulletins) to Governing Board members who were leaving for a cigarette or bathroom break. Right away we were accused of being pushy. Ecumenical etiquette crashing. Some strategy. Who knew?

But back to that opening worship service. Suddenly, sitting in the last aisle in that huge church, I realized some things. The NCC and I were (are) the same age (we were both 31 at the time). I thought of all it had taken to bring us together at this moment in history. Suddenly, I sensed them in the room: gay men and lesbians through the ages. In the churches, burned by the churches, persecuted by the churches, serving the churches, loving and hurting. They were there. They knew I was there. I had this overwhelming sense of a mystical communion of gay and lesbian saints, some of whom had served this council in its better days. I wept for them and for us, for their longing, pain and shame, for their need even now for vindication and for a voice. And I felt so small, and young, and inadequate. But also so loved and watched over by them. From that moment until this, they have never left me. And many thousands have been added to their numbers.

Then everyone stood together and sang a song I had loved a long time, the text written by an angry, questioning son of the Church:

> *Once to every [soul] and nation*
> *Comes the moment to decide*

27

*In the strife of truth with falsehood,*
*For the good or evil side....*
*Then it is the brave [one] chooses,*
*While the coward stands aside,*
*Till the multitude make virtue*
*Of the faith they had denied.*

*By the light of burning martyrs,[6]*
*Christ, Thy bleeding feet we track,*
*Toiling up new Calvaries ever*
*With the cross that turns not back;*
*New occasions teach new duties,*
*Time makes ancient good uncouth;*
*They must upward still, and onward, who would*
*Keep abreast of truth.*

James Russell Lowell

The NCC were singing our song! But did they know it yet? And, oh, *they* were also singing right along with us. The presence of my heavenly tribe sustained me that day and in every NCC governing board since.

Later on in the NCC adventure, we held three "consultations." One of these was on "Biblical Issues and Homosexuality." One of the presenters was Dr. Robin Scroggs, a New Testament Pauline scholar. He is a heterosexual scholar who has been willing to take another look at the traditional passages in Paul that have been used to condemn homosexuality and homosexuals. One of Dr. Scroggs's theses is that the New Testament simply doesn't address the situation of contemporary gay and lesbian people because in his opinion, male homosexual relationships were in New Testament times all pederastic. In the midst of that meeting, it suddenly occurred to me that he might be suggesting that there were no ancient gay men and lesbians who had mutually consenting adult relationships. When I asked him if that was what he meant, he paused, then said, "Yes."

"How do you know that?" I asked.

His argument was one of silence. I felt this horror and rage in me that could not shut up. How could he just say that there were no people like me, like us, of our tribe, in those times? How dare he say that! And how unfortunate to argue from silence.

But more than that, I had to ask myself, "How do I know we were there?" Judy Grahn has certainly documented us (and not as pederasts, either) in ancient history, folklore, mythology and literature. But how did I know that day? I realized that I knew it in my guts. In my heart, in my body, and blood, and spirit, and wherever else it is that we just know things. The heavenly tribe was there, some of whom preceded New Testament times. They knew. And they now had a way of getting my attention. Dr. Scroggs's remark, his theories, seemed harmless enough on the surface. But to me they were something akin to historical genocide. I felt all this terrible grief at the suggestion that they (we) had not been there all along. Closeted, for sure. Quiet, oppressed and silent, but there.

Israel, too, had a complex process of identity formation. Who are the Jews? Are they a race or a tribe, a religion or a nation, a culture or a set of traditions? They are a people with a vague prehistory. They were shaped by the historical crucibles of the Exodus and Exile; by courageous leaders; common oppression; covenant values; by storytellers and events. They were forged from an amalgam of tribes and peoples.

What name would we, did we call those who would want to dissect a Jewish hypothalamus? "Nazi," I think. So how come our collective hypothalami are so dissectable? So terribly interesting? For those of us who long for sexual orientation to be not our fault (something like diabetes), the hypothalamus thing must seem like an enormous relief. But I am skeptical, to say the least. What creates community? What creates tribe? Why do some tribes last, some don't, some disappear into the mists of time?

There is a certain critical tension about this *tribal identity thing.* I remember reading death-of-God theologian Richard Rubenstein's book *After Auschwitz* when I was in college. I recall his searching questions about the implications of the Jewish concept of *chosenness*, its permutations in Christian thought, and the terribly twisted notions of chosenness that characterized the Nazi doctrine of Aryan supremacy. He asked if the concept of chosenness, no matter how humble or benign, might lead inevitably to doctrines of exclusiveness and superiority. To many, of course, Rubenstein's critique sounded all too much like blaming the victim. However, his critique of what I call "tribal ontology" is perhaps more relevant than ever in these days of global ethnic conflicts and growing fundamentalism. The dilemma of tribal theology and tribal biblical hermeneutics is discussed at length in the book *Out of Every Tribe and Nation* by Justo

Gonzales.[7] On the one hand, "there is always the likelihood that any theology that claims to be universal is no more than theology from the particular perspective of those who are in power."[8] In other words, the dominant tribes set the agenda, and get to "universalize" their tribal theology. On the other hand there is the danger of what he calls the romanticization of culture in which groups may "idealize [their] culture as if it were perfect and did not stand in need of correction from the gospel."[9] No culture is free from human problems and divisions. There has to be a delicate balance between the search for the universal and the context of tribal particularism. We must acknowledge that we live in a world of shifting hierarchies—and for some of us, they don't shift fast enough!

So, do gay and lesbian people identify more with our tribe(s) or more with our humanness? Does our tribal identification give us the courage and strength to claim our humanness? Or does it urge us to compare ourselves, to judge ourselves as worse or better than others? Those in whatever dominant group or culture always want all the rest of us to focus on our generic humanness, on how alike we are, not on our differences. Is the notion of generic humanness essentially classist, racist, sexist?[10]

Only 25 years ago, Rev. Troy Perry had to write, in an open letter to the church (from *The Lord Is My Shepherd and He* [sic] *Knows I'm Gay*), "I am not a creature from the other darkness, I am a man of flesh and blood."[11] In many places in the world, it is our humanness as gays and lesbians that is still the issue.

I met Kiron (not his real name), a gay East Indian man, the way I have met many people over the years. His lover, Jerry, was dying of AIDS. Jerry's parents stayed in Kiron and Jerry's home in Los Angeles during Jerry's final days. Jerry's mother, in fact, lived there for months. Kiron cared for Jerry until he had to go to the hospital. Jerry's parents were never openly rude to Kiron, but he knew they had never approved of Jerry's lifestyle. Nevertheless, Kiron showed them every kindness, gave them a key to his home, was very hospitable. The day after Jerry died, Kiron went to work in his law office as usual. He was not out to his colleagues or clerical staff and felt he could not risk being absent from work, even the day after his lover of six years had died.

When he returned home that night, the apartment felt strange. Then he realized that Jerry's parents had left. And they had taken many things. All of Jerry's possessions but not only that: they had stolen things that had belonged to both of them. Precious photographs, personal effects.

Kiron collapsed in grief and rage. In order for these good, churchgoing folks to do such a thing, they had to be willing to see Kiron as less than human, not deserving of ordinary human courtesy and respect, much less gratitude. They had to be willing to negate all the evidence of the love and commitment between their son and this gentle, good man. Kiron never saw Jerry's parents or any of his things again.[12]

This tension between our tribal and our human identity is a difficult issue for gay men, lesbians and bisexuals.

I met Chris Cowap in 1974 at the first meeting of the NCC's Commission on Women in Ministry. It was an incredible gathering of about 120 or so powerful women church leaders and feminists. My invitation was a last-minute one, thanks to Roy Birchard, pastor of Metropolitan Community Church of New York who doubled as a secretary for the Presbyterians at the "God Box" (a term of affection for the Inter-Church Center, 475 Riverside Drive in Manhattan). I got a "gay underground" invitation, which meant that I would never know precisely how I got invited.

I was 23 at the time and still at MCC Boston, and I was the only out lesbian at this meeting. Just by showing up, I evidently caused quite a stir, and people went out of their way to either greet me or avoid me. By the end of the weekend, after dozens of midnight tearful conversations and hallway comings-out, I'd guess that nearly one-third of those women were dykes or well on their way. It was an exhilarating and exhausting introduction to the world of ecumenical feminism of the '70s.

But of all of them, Chris probably affected me the most. An intense, politically savvy lay Episcopalian, career social-justice ecumenist, Chris was already an instant hero to me. When she wanted to speak to me, I was flattered and curious. She just looked at me, shook her head, and said tearfully, "I'm just never going to be able to do it."

"Do what?" I asked. (Duh.)

"Come out, like you." Chris was a dyke! Well, of course. She just kept shaking her head. She told me about her activism in the civil rights movement, her feminist identification, her commitment to progressive environmental causes and to human rights. But, she said, "I can't do this last thing. I can't do this last thing that is really for and about me. And I'm ashamed. When I look at you, I'm ashamed. I'm ashamed I can't do it for myself and that I can't be more supportive of you." I remember just holding her a while and thanking her for coming out to me. I tried to reassure her that I *did* feel supported, just by her *human* example.

From time to time after that, whenever I was in New York, I would try to find Chris while minimizing the danger of exposing her. She moved around in the God Box quite a bit, first to the WCC and then later back to the NCC. I remember sneaking up to her office with Rev. Karen Ziegler, trying to be invisible on the way! ("Nah, I didn't just see two dykes sneaking by into Chris's office, did you?") Chris always looked glad to see me, and the feeling was mutual. Plus she possessed a wealth of knowledge about everything ecumenical. She was my inside track.

Through the ecumenical feminist grapevine I eventually heard about her lung cancer. When we applied for membership in the NCC in 1981, Chris had just gone into remission and was just coming back to work. Seeing her at those meetings was wonderful. She provided great support to us in those days. And eventually around the AIDS issue.

In early November 1983, on the way to the Hartford meeting of the NCC during which they would be voting on our eligibility for membership, Chris tracked me down at my brother's home in Indianapolis. I had stopped by Indianapolis for three reasons. Most importantly, to do my youngest brother's wedding at a large Methodist church. My parents and family would be there. Also, I wanted to have one last chance at a conversation with Bishop Armstrong, whose office happened to be in Indianapolis.

Third, I had had a troubling dream about a former student clergy of mine who had been pastoring MCC in Louisville, Kentucky. I had not seen Sandy in several years, and I missed her and was worried about her. I asked her to come to Indianapolis while I was there.

My conversation with Bishop Armstrong was extremely discouraging. He seemed scattered and hostile, as well he might have been only one week away from his surprise resignation as president of the NCC. And I did get to see my friend Sandy. For a few precious hours a few of us gathered in a little bar on the outskirts of Indianapolis. It would be the last time I would ever see her. She died three weeks later, probably from suicide. We will never know for sure.

But Chris managed to track me down. I liked that. I had always attributed a certain omniscience to her, and this only reinforced it. She opened with "I'm gonna do it!"

"Do what?" (Duh, again.)

"Come out." She said she figured there had to be a reason for all this cancer remission stuff. And this must be it. (Chris always skipped formalities in conversations with me. She talked as if we had spoken just yesterday and not six months ago.) She told me that if the NCC turned MCC down for eligibility or membership, she would publicly come out at the meeting in Hartford. All I could think of was our first meeting and how Chris thought she could never do it. She had been a person for all people but not quite a person for herself. And perhaps now that was about to change. No longer a generic person, Chris could claim her lesbian self.

The Hartford NCC meeting was a zoo. The *Inclusive Language Lectionary* was being introduced. Dr. Virginia Ramey Mollenkott, a member of the committee, infuriated some of her colleagues by coming out at that meeting, in support of MCC. The Lectionary Committee had excited so much attention from the press and religious conservatives that our issue seemed overshadowed at times. The committee had, in fact, been subjected to harassing phone calls and even death threats that had necessitated calling in the FBI. The NCC received much more negative mail about the lectionary than it ever received about us in 11 years. But they still published the lectionary, which many of us in UFMCC use. It always mystified me that the NCC practiced such selective courage.

After days of ecu-political machinations, the die was cast. A poorly written "compromise" motion was adopted that would *postpone indefinitely* their vote on our eligibility for membership. They couldn't say yes, but they couldn't say no either. This would become something of a dysfunctional pattern in the UFMCC/NCC relationship, the "come here/go away" version of ecu-teasing: "We can't bear to think of ourselves as rejecting you, so we'll just call it something else and keep everyone guessing." Except the cynics, of course, who knew all along.

When the vote happened, I was immediately called out into the hallway in front of 50 or 60 reporters, TV cameras, microphones, and so on to read our prepared statement, putting a cautiously optimistic spin on it all. We queers were good sports in those days. Speaking of sports Dr. Eileen Lindner, NCC staffer in those days, (later to become Associate General Secretary) told me that the *Hartford Currant* was short-staffed that day, and sent it's sports reporter(!) to cover the MCC story. The reporter asked her, "So, let me understand this—it's the guys in the skirts (the Orthodox) who don't want to let the queers in?"

Meanwhile, Chris sat in her seat in the assembly room, a little numb and confused. She had a prearranged signal with Dr. Jane Carey Peck, Professor of Ethics at Andover Newton School of Theology and on the

United Methodist delegation to the governing board of the NCC. If the vote was negative, Chris would stand, and Jane Carey would look for her and yield the floor to her. (As a member of the staff, Chris did not automatically have a voice at the Governing Board meeting.) The only problem was that when the vote happened, Chris was not sure just how negative it was, and she sat there, trying to decide. Then as she told Virginia Mollenkott and me later that evening, she suddenly felt two hands on her shoulders lifting her out of her seat. When she turned around to see who had done it, no one was there.

Jane Carey got the signal and yielded the floor to Chris. The room was utterly still. Someone came running out into the hallway to get me, saying, "Chris is at the mike!" I ran into the meeting room in time to hear this:

DR. JANE CAREY PECK: Jane Carey Peck, United Methodist. I ask for a point of personal privilege in order to yield the floor to a staff member of the Division of Church and Society, one of the valued and leading contributors to our common work, Chris Cowap.

CHRIS COWAP: I don't want to be here. And I don't have any choice. Dr. Lois Wilson said this morning that "to be a person is to be relational; that's what defines us." I want to define myself in her terms.

I am a daughter; I am a sister; I am an aunt; I'm a friend; I'm a colleague; for almost ten years now I've been a servant in this community of the council; and I'm a woman who loves another woman. And I'm sure with every fiber of my being that I am a child of God and an inheritor of the kingdom of heaven.

When I have felt God's judgment on me—and I have, too many times—it has never been because of the nature of those relationships. It's been because I have allowed them or caused them to be broken, to be not-love.

I said I don't want to be here—right here—and yet I feel compelled right now by the Holy Spirit to be here, saying this. I hear this: not a heavenly choir but a single voice, singing "Hodie! This is the day, Chris, when you must, in love, assert in this community in which you have been called to serve, to these brothers and sisters in Christ with whom you have been in com-

34

munity, you must affirm Cod's affirmation of you. You can't do anything else." This has not simply been an institutional matter, and you know that I am not speaking as one lone individual. I'm not speaking as a spokesperson; I wasn't chosen as a spokesperson. But you know that there are other people in this room—in the choir lofts, in the sacristies, in the pews, in the seminaries, in your national staffs—for whom I am speaking. I believe that you honestly intend, some of you, to continue in the dialogue and to wrestle with prayer and continued pain with the questions of what it means to be human and what it means to be truly members of one another. And you need to know that there are some of us who feel called by God to be here and to stay here to be in that kind of dialogue with you." [13]

Chris Cowap died four and a half years later of lung cancer. In the years between 1983 and 1988, I had the privilege of rooming with Chris several times at NCC meetings. We never talked about it (she was always curt and businesslike), so I don't know which of us got the bigger kick out of watching people trying *not* to wonder just what was "going on." Mostly what was going on was that Chris would regale me (and sometimes Sandy Robinson, president of MCC's Samaritan College) with wonderful feminist ecumenical folklore. She especially loved to tell Claire Randall stories. While drinking her white wine, Chris (who was mostly bald from chemotherapy) would take off her wig and NCC drag, don her dykish white T-shirt, and talk, and talk, and talk.

And sometimes we touched. Like the time she was in such excruciating pain (from the progressing cancer) that I had her lie on her side while I laid hands on her chest and back, doing light massage and heavy prayer.

Chris eventually succumbed. But not before she had resolved in herself that terrible tension between her commitment to all people and all the earth and her commitment to her own special and lovely tribe. When they (the heavenly members of the tribe) put their hands on her that afternoon in Hartford, lifting her out of her seat, then helped her to do what had seemed so remote and utterly impossible only nine years before.

I must also thank God for dear Jane Carey, who died of ovarian cancer in 1990. I always wondered if she saw just who it was that stood behind Chris that day in Hartford.

In many ways, the ecumenical movement is the only other "church" in which I have ever felt completely at home besides MCC. It has been a source of some of my most powerful spiritual experiences and deepest friendships.

In 1991, I had the privilege of serving as MCC's delegate observer to the World Council of Churches General Assembly in Canberra, Australia. The first Sunday we were there we shared the very first celebration of the Lima liturgy[14] at a WCC assembly. This was the first chance for this worldwide ecumenical assembly to celebrate communion with the carefully crafted and negotiated words. Even the Eastern Orthodox agreed on the wording of the liturgy. The only barrier was that they, and some others, could still not agree on who was legitimately able to preside over communion. So it was still far from perfect, and incomplete as an ecumenical Eucharist. Nevertheless, the celebration went forward that day, with 5,000 or so in attendance under that big, open tent under the big, open Australian summer sky. Outside, conservative Eastern Orthodox people protested the celebration, criticizing Orthodox ecumenists with huge, vilifying signs. I think some fundamentalist critics were there, too.

The liturgy was breathtakingly gorgeous. Aboriginal participation hallowed the ground and space; the processional was grand. A young, tall, adorable lesbian with a buzz haircut towered above the other processors. I noticed her right away. Steve Pieters, Kit Cherry, and I poked each other with the "We are everywhere!" poke.

Then came the invitation to communion, and people began to do just as we do in UFMCC, to stream forward down the aisle, mostly single file, to receive the holy elements. Other than Kit and Steve, I knew no one else in our section of the tent. I probably knew only about 200 of the 5,000 there that day. Suddenly, I was overwhelmed. I saw the faces of hundreds and hundreds of strangers streaming down the aisles, hungry and thirsty, hardly a dry eye. We were all aware of the beauty and pain and historicity of this moment. And then it seemed to me that I actually knew all of these strangers. They looked just like people I served communion to every Sunday at MCC Los Angeles. Well, not just like, but very close. All races, nations, sizes, shapes, sexualities, ages.

I am always amazed at what happens to tired, older, dry, craggy adult faces when they come to communion. How faces soften, open, even glow. How older people start to look younger. Wide-eyed, open, trusting, needy. Unashamed. It was as if I knew every person who streamed forward. Suddenly it was as if I could have told you, if you had asked me, not only every name but every story, their fears, dreams, how they "got over" (a Mahalia Jackson song), how they got there. I began to cry, something I did very infrequently in those days. I remembered Søren Kierkegaard's words to the effect that if we *knew everything* about a person—their pain, fears, losses, loves—we could not help but love them to death.

Suddenly, proud to be representing my tribe, I was transported to a posttribal reality. It no longer mattered, everything was dissolving. Especially me. Never in all my life had I experienced the sense of overpowering connectedness to the earth and all her people. And then it shifted just a little bit more. I was a child in a huge family gathering. Somehow along the way I had lost contact with my parents, which was very frightening. But there was this deep consolation, because all the folks around me had this vague family resemblance that made me feel safe, at home. Just like the ways my Aunt Betty and Aunt Jo looked enough like my mom so that just seeing them always made me feel secure, like it would all be all right somehow. If I lost my parents, my family, my tribal connections of whatever type, I was still safe in the arms of this extended tribal network. Now my tears were of belonging and relief.

I'm not sure how long that experience lasted. Eventually I got up and made my way forward to the most ecumenical Eucharist the world had experienced to date, probably since the first century. Me and my gay and lesbian tribe partook with the rest. One Body. One Blood.

Fast Forward seven years to 1998. After a long period of rocky relations with the US National Council of Churches, and quietly preparing to go to Zimbabwe for the last General Assembly of the World Council of Churches in the 20th century, all hell began to break lose in the world of gays and lesbians in ecumenicism, again, along with some terrific breakthroughs.

On top of all the AIDS deaths, and horrific losses we had experienced over a decade, I lost my ecumical staff person in 1995. Kit Cherry, a author in her own right, got very ill with a mysterious, hard-to-diagnose illness, and, after struggling could not return to work. That was a heartbreaking, disappointing, and painful time for many of us who knew and worked with Kit.

But in 1997, I began working with a bright, energetic, middle-aged seminarian, Dr. Gwynne Guibord, who is a natural born ecumenist, singleminded, creative, opinionated and determined. She broke through some of my lethargy (and UFMCC's) about ecumenism, and started making great local strides in California. She addressed the U.S. National Council of Churches in late 1998, and began pioneering historic new alliances.

At the same time, we began envisioning a team going to Harare, Zimbabwe, since all those who had gone with me to Canberra, to the last Assembly were no longer working at headquarters, had become ill, moved on or died. We needed to put together a team, including Africans, Europeans, women and men, a multi-racial team.

From the beginning, we had a lot of friction. Some of that was in the context of major staff changes at headquarters, after a period of conflict and disruption. Gwynne, who was still a volunteer at that time, was very focused on building our connection to the WCC itself, making them take us seriously as a church, positioning ourselves to be a part of the Assembly. Others wanted to go primarily to evangelize and offer witness to the ministry of MCC, to recruit, to support GALZ (Gays and Lesbians of Zimbabwe). Others were a little frightened of what we night encounter there, with a lethally homophobic President, Robert Mugabe, who had compared homosexuals to dogs.

Some staff members were urging caution, others were ready to "act up." As always, I tended to see all sides, and to embrace more than one strategy, while trying to keep the team together, or at least from undermining each other. I was never completely successful, and tensions continued throughout the year, and through the Assembly itself.

Gwynne and I went to Geneva in November of 1998 to meet with General Secretary Konrad Raiser, at his invitation. The WCC, especially their gay and gay-friendly staff, were trying to head off a big collision in Harare. In fact, they met with GALZ, they met with Mugabe, they met with gay-friendly denominations of the Council, they did a lot of excellent preparation work. Konrad Raiser spoke movingly and very frankly about his encounter with Mugabe, and how firm he had to be about the WCC's insistence that we would have to be able to talk openly about the issue of homosexuality. They even got a written agreement from Mugabe stating the those attending the WCC Assembly would not be harassed, and that there could be free speech for the duration of the proceedings.

Even with that, the WCC officials were worried. Just weeks before the Assembly, GALZ was uninvited to offer a workshop at the Padare, the "workshop fair" being held on campus as an adjunct program of the Assembly, intended to be a place where "hot button" and difficult issues could be safely addressed in a non-parliamentary setting. They had been invited to offer a workshop, but the sponsoring denomination had withdrawn their support at the last minute, which, according to the rules, meant they were not legally authorized to participate.

I think the WCC overreacted. I believe they should have just said it was too late to uninvite GALZ, and gone ahead and let them do their workshop. That would have been the less disruptive course, I think. Instead, by uninviting GALZ, people from all over the world began running to their defense and rescue. Especially since Mugabe's relentless homophobic rhetoric had been reported in the *New York Times*, and other international media.

Several other delegations, including UFMCC, the United Church of Christ, USA, the Dutch delegations, the United Church of Canada and other Canadians and South Africans invited GALZ to participate in their workshops. WCC staffers "secured" day passes for GALZ members over the objections of some. UFMCC took up an offering for GALZ at the official worship service we held at the Assembly. This galvanized gay and lesbian participants, and our allies.

Of the nearly 1000 delegates, only two or three of us were official delegates that were openly gay or lesbian, and all of us were in the bleachers in that stifling auditorium at the University of Harare. The rest of the nearly 100 openly lesbian and gay attendees to the Assembly were "visitors," and had to watch the proceedings from tents outside, with 4000 other visitors from around the world.

Louie Crew, from Integrity U.S., and myself, chaired the nightly "queer" meetings over the two week period of the Assembly. Louie was our leader. He was amazing with his energy, ideas, his gentle persistence, his humor. Every night we met with Representatives of GALZ, while the "CIA counterpart" of Zimbabwe also attended our meetings. They were painfully obvious, and Louie took great delight in camping it up while addressing them, from time to time, throughout our meetings.

The first night we were not laughing. None of us knew what was going to happen. In fact, were we told not to bring any gay or lesbian literature into the country, that we might be stopped at immigration, etc. However, I think the Zimbabwe immigration officials were quite busy enough and overwhelmed with all these church folks coming in, and it was probably hard to tell which of these Westerners were the queer ones, if they thought about it at all.

That first night we listened to GALZ members tell their stories. I asked MCC members (notably, Estella Thomas, known as "E.T.") to stand guard outside the door. Every time a new person came in (40-50 people crammed into a classroom), we would tense up a little. But, gradually, as we met night after night, we relaxed. We moved into the open visitors tent for our meetings. We relaxed. We got used to the "undercover" police and just took them into account every meeting.

Every day, the Assembly managed to avoid ever mentioning the word "homosexuality" or "Gay," while every day at the press Conference, it was the main topic of discussion. Jim Birkett from UFMCC and the indominable Richard Kirker from the Gay Christian Movement in England were also at press meetings every day. Richard was tireless, and, I know, a thorn in the side of the WCC, at times. I loved strategizing with him. He relished his journalistic role, and was scrupulous about his journalistic ethics. He was having the time of his life, rooming with two Zimbabwean lesbians who earned their living by giving tours of Harare to tourists (including WCC tourists, in some twist of queer irony).

Even when the report of the Ecumencal Decade in Solidarity with Women came up on the floor of the Assembly, they wouldn't read the report aloud, because of the language in the document that courageously (though subtly) acknowledged the work and presence of lesbians at the conference; and that acknowledged the difficulties churches were having dealing with the issue of sexual orientation. It was Gwynne, attending the week long women's meeting before the conference, who had provided the wording and fought for the issue to be named and included. But the issue "dared not speak it's name" at the assembly until the very last day, when the press had gone home. Even on the issue of Human Rights, any references to gay and lesbian human rights were eliminated. The issue of our humanness is still, apparently, not a settled one. Only Dr. Paul Sherry, from the United Church of Christ, rose to object to our non-inclusion with passion and eloquence, as usual.

Finally, some kind of study process was authorized, and the WCC has us on their agenda for this millennium.

But the tension between the "formal" proceedings and the rest of the Assembly was astonishing. Rainbow ribbons proliferated, and everywhere people were buzzing about us, about "it."

Daily, GALZ was courageous and visible. Keith Goddard, a GALZ leader, a frail, small man with a curved spine and twinkling eyes, was my hero. He was fearless, a joyful warrior, having sued the government of Zimbabwe when the police destroyed GALZ's booth at a public bookfair years before. And he won. Sitting next to him, and other GALZ leaders that first night in Zimbabwe filled me with awe.

Keith presided over a lively human rights, community service organization, Gays and Lesbians of Zimbabwe (GALZ) that was everything to everyone. A heterosexual woman cochaired GALZ with him. Lesbians were very involved in the day to day operations, but, as in every culture, are much less visible. GALZ leased a large house that they were trying to purchase. It served as a bar, disco, barbecue and picnic place, a shelter for people who had been kicked out of their homes, a counselling center, a center for activism. Drag queens were everywhere. In some ways, it was a lot like the '70s in the US. But different: they have been facing a virulently homophobic President, who is losing his political power, and blaming students, unions and homosexuals for the woes of the country. Keith has recently been imprisoned and consistently lives in danger. The GALZ center has been abandoned.

We all worked hard those weeks, meeting as many people as we could. Our South African delegates staffed the booth. E.T. from MCC L.A., hovered over us , managed our transportation, ran all over campus, kept track of everyone. Rev. Judy Dahl, Global Outreach Director of UFMCC worked tirelessly meeting with people interested in starting MCC's in their countries. We ordained one of our South African pastors, Daniel Botha, while we are were there, at a moving service in a little meeting room at the hotel.

Elder Hong Tan from London preached a fiery coming out/human rights sermon at the UFMCC worship service we provided during the Padare. It was the only time communion was offered at the Assembly. Margarita Sanches de Leon, from MCC in Puerto Rico, hooked up with her UCC friends, especially those from the Caribbean, and interfaced with those involved in human rights worldwide.

I was assigned to a small group for ten days. The groups met in little tents, on the muddy grounds of the University of Harere. When I finally found the tent, I nearly gasped when I entered. In the group sat all men. And, not just any men: A Coptic Orthodox Bishop, a Bishop who headed the Church of Pakistan, the head of a German church, the Bishop who

leads the Church of Sweden, a University Professor from the Syrian Orthodox Church in India...and me.

We all smiled politely, and introduced ourselves. I let them know I
was (by that time) the vice moderator of MCC worldwide, which makes
me a Bishop equivalent, I guess. I told them very matter of factly about
MCC's outreach. Some of them sucked in their breath, narrowed their
eyes. Some, I could tell, hadn't quite heard me or understood. The German fellow never came back. I alternately love and hate having that kind
of power.

But I didn't make a big deal of it. We did our Bible study for an hour
and a half. It was lively. At the end of our first session, the professor from
India and the Coptic Bishop walked with me and began to interrogate me.
They thought I was a compassionate straight woman who was helping
those poor homosexuals. So, I had to keep coming out and coming out,
and they kept looking at me, surprised, scandalized. If America was the
promiscuous place they knew it to be, why, they reasoned, would people
need to "resort" to homosexual sex? This was a new twist on an old theme
for me. I smiled, and told them , you know, there are just some people
who prefer homosexual sex. "No!" they said, mouths open, shaking their
heads. They said, "we have no such people in our countries or cultures—
except criminals." I told them, "Yes you do. They are just secretive, underground, unable to be open." "Really," they said, quite sincerely incredulous.

We met every day. At first, we never talked about me, or UFMCC, or
sexuality in the group. We did the Bible study. I was low key. We talked a
lot about Christianity in Muslim countries. I learned a lot about what it
means to be a religious minority. They were very open and eager to talk
to me. Gradually, they began including me, and my situation in their conversations. After every Bible study, our walks back to the main area for
lunch would get more and more lively and interesting. We talked about
sex, gay marriage, youth, what our church services are like. They were
insatiably curious.

When the General Assembly erupted in a debate over polygamy, our
small group got even more lively. I turned the tables on them, and asked
these presumably heterosexual men about the real situation in their cultures and churches. They talked about adultery, divorce and problems.
Some confessed they thought polygamy actually worked better in their
cultures, though they would never dare say this in their churches. One

42

even said his brother in law was "homophobic." A week before he had denied that there was homosexuality in his culture. Now he spoke of a homophobic brother in law! It was amazing. They were embarrassed, at first, to be honest with me about heterosexual sexual struggles. But, they loosened up, they got into it, arguing and debating.

It wasn't as civil at the Assembly itself when the issue of polygamy arose. When the Membership Committee recommended a church for membership which still had some remnant of polygamous practice, the Assembly balked. Clearly, the new members and clergy of the applicant church were committed to practicing and teaching monogamy, but they didn't want to tell men to divorce their wives and abandon them. Even the Catholic Church doesn't require that. But the Assembly refused to accept the church, even though there are member churches of the council who already are in that same situation. The difficult part was that people clapped when the church was rejected. That stunned me and made me glad they weren't voting on our application that day.

The General Secretary, Dr. Raiser, was visibly shaken. The next day, in his singularly most passionate statement of the Assembly, he chastised the crowd for the unkindness of rejoicing at the rejection of a church that applied in good faith to belong to the council. I flashed back and flashed forward a lot during his brief but pointed remarks. I was grateful for his willingness to set a tone of civility in the face of difficult issues. He may need to do that again in the future, I thought.

By the end of our two weeks, our Bible Study group was talking about all kinds of issues. My presence became quite "normalized," although my presence had also transformed the group. And, I, who had been dreading meeting with people I was sure would be closed minded, was humbled and pleased to end up feeling so close to these men.

Before the time together ended, I was invited to India. And, I invited the Pakistani Bishop to preach at my church when he visited Los Angeles. I was interviewed by a reporter from an Indian women's magazine that reached millions of women.

My professor friend took both my hands in his the last day, looked me in the eyes and said "I owe you an apology. Prior to this I thought of homosexuals as criminals, as antisocial, You are about as far from antisocial as I can imagine. I promise you I will work to change the homophobia in my University, my city, my country. Thank you."

While Gwynne worked with the WCC Staff on our presentations,

43

others reached out to potential MCC pastors, closeted gay folk, and resistant straight people who wanted to know what these rainbows were all about. Others dealt with the press. UFMCC hosted a press conference off campus with GALZ, and gay rights activists from South Africa, Namibia, Zambia and other places spoke. We had a fabulous reception at the GALZ headquarters, and partied, and danced and prayed. Judy Dahl worked on making a stronger, permanent UFMCC Zimbabwe connection, especially through the South Africans MCCers, notably Rev. Sue Wellman, and Rev. Paul Mokete. Later in the week, Gwynne went with other Americans to the U.S. Ambassador's home to plead for support for human rights for GALZ and homosexual Zimbabweans.

And we prayed. Elder Hong Tan lead a prayer vigil outside the Assembly hall the day Robert Mugabe attended the Assembly. We were all agitated about it. Since only a handful of us were in the Assembly hall, we had to strategize. Hong decided to lead a prayer vigil outside. The night before, MCCers took bedsheets and made a sign for me to unveil, should it be needed. I folded the sign, which simple said, "GOD LOVES ALL PEOPLE", and folded it in my bookbag. As I entered the hall, I noticed scores of Zimbabwean soldiers with rifles in every corner of the auditorium. Young, thin, soldiers, eyes darting everywhere. I went to my usual post in the balcony, after connecting with Paul Sherry, and Simon Mgoli, an openly gay Tasmanian delegate. If Mugabe said anything homophobic, or against GALZ, I would lean over the balcony and unfurl the banner.

By the time I made my way to my seat I realized that making a commotion in the balcony could cause a reaction from those young, heavily armed soldiers. I knew it was risky. And I prayed. Mostly I prayed that the moment would pass. I would not hesitate to unfurl the banner, but I was uncomfortable with the fact that it might have consequences I couldn't control.

If Mugabe said anything, he would be doing it to show he wasn't intimidated by the WCC. If he didn't say anything, it would be because he really did get their message that his homophobia was not welcomed in the Assembly.

Mugabe had been scheduled to speak several time, but had not come earlier in the Assembly. He had been shopping in London. Many people complained about Mugabe, and the rumor was that he had spent less than two weeks all year in his own country during very difficult economic and political times.

When he entered the hall, they played the national anthem of Zimbabwe, and I reluctantly stood, wanting to honor the country, but not thrilled to honor Comrade Mugabe. After a fairly lengthy speech, he started to talk about family values. I moved to the balcony. He hesitated, actually stopped for a moment, as if deciding...and moved on. I knew the moment had passed. I refolded my sheet, and in the middle of an unsatisfied adrenaline rush, walked back to my seat in the bleachers.

After Mugabe finished speaking, AME Bishop, and WCC President Vinton Anderson responded, in a very formal, traditional way. He did take the time to chide Mugabe a bit about the need to make better progress in human rights. In what I thought was a thinly veiled reference to Mugabe's religiously based (he's Catholic) homophobia, he talked about the need to respect all human beings, because "God loves all people." I felt tears sting in my eyes as I heard Bishop Anderson say the simple words on my banner for me. It was such a confirmation of the Holy Spirit, and I took it very personally. I'm sure some people missed the point of his message. I'm sure Mugabe did not.

Later, as the press moved in on Mugabe as he left the Assembly, no longer under WCC civility restraints, he spewed off a few choice homophobic remarks. (Keith Goddard, of GALZ, had predicted this, and was disgusted, feeling the WCC had been duped into giving support to Mugabe.) Mugabe's comments were the parting, cowardly shots of a person who has lost the respect of the world and of many of his own people.

I knew unfurling that banner would have made a great photo opportunity, and a little part of me regrets not doing it anyway, though, if it had not been in the context of a specific homophobic remark, most people would not have understood it. On the other hand, I wasn't into getting shot or risking getting others shot for a "photo op."

Some had predicted that this would be the last WCC assembly, but I think not. There will be more opportunities for the Church to reconcile and heal. And we will be there.

# Chapter One—Healing
# Our Tribal Wounds

The religious right in the United States (now often called the "religious wrong" by some) is fond of going on and on about the *gay agenda*. Oh, that we were as well organized as they fantasize! I believe that we must have a tribal agenda. Two urgent components of that agenda are *healing our tribal wounds* and *boldly exercising our tribal gifts*.

I have had the privilege and soul-stirring challenge of working with Dr. Mel White, whose organization SoulForce seeks to use the principles of Jesus, Ghandi and Martin Luther King to try to confront the source of our tribal wounds in the hateful rhetoric of the Religious Right. Mel is a member of MCC Los Angeles and an MCC minister, who, with his partner Gary Nixon, is a tireless and passionate champion of gay and lesbian nonviolence, and author of *Stranger at the Gate*.

Mel's theory is that we need to stop the violence at the source. I'm not sure I agree the Religious Right is the source of our wounds—rather, it is the source of religious homophobia. In many ways, I think that the Roman Catholic Church and other religious groups are also part of that source, even those who could never be called the Religious Right. Homophobia is older, deeper and broader than fundamentalism, but fundamentalism and the Right wing have surely used homophobia to raise money and interest in their agendas. I think the roots of homophobia are in misogyny. And, while the Religious Right is patriarchal and misogynist, it did not invent those pathologies, not did it invent homophobia.

Speaking of agendas, lifting the ban on gays and lesbians in the military in the United States was not really at the top of the charts in terms of the agenda for the gay or lesbian organizations in the 1990s. And yet, in the early days of the Clinton campaign and presidency, it surfaced as a key issue. The reasons for the issue surfacing, and the ambivalence of the gay and lesbian community and leadership about the issue are complicated, and have been written about elsewhere. To generalize, a lot of the gay and lesbian establishment in our country have been baby boomers, some of whom were antiwar activists in the '60s and '70s, and they were not willing to portray gay and lesbians as pro-military or patriotic.

Yet history and circumstances pushed this issue to the top when Bill Clinton was elected President. The idea that many gay and lesbian people have a deep, unfulfilled desire to join the military is patently ridiculous. Yet, there are many gay and lesbian veterans, and of gays and lesbian soldiers currently serving with honor. Something about the psychology and sociology of minority group legitimacy in the American mind is related to military status. It seems to be the test of "true citizenship," which in political currency is the same thing as "humanness."

This came home to me at the funeral of an older African American gay clergyman who had been on the staff of MCC Los Angeles for many years, who died not long after Clinton came into office. Thomas Walker was a gentle, beloved man who had devoted his ministry to helping alcoholics like himself. I do not remember knowing before his death that Thomas was also a navy veteran.

I presided over his funeral, which was attended by many of his family, by the pastor of their congregation (Progress Baptist Church, Compton, California), and by many MCC people and members of Alcoholics Anonymous. Thomas, in his death, had assembled a very eclectic group. As we bid him farewell at the end of the funeral and after the last "Amen," the director of the funeral home, as is customary at the funerals of veterans, gave an American flag to the family. We were gathered in the lower level of the mausoleum in which Thomas was being buried. I had forgotten about this final bit of funeral procedure. As the funeral director took the flag to present it to Thomas's brother, he said something like "On behalf of the President of the United States, a grateful nation presents this flag to you." Grief cracked open like a huge egg, at least for the MCC L.A. folks. I thought about how many times I had been at the funerals of veterans. The words had always seemed like an afterthought, even an intrusion. But context is everything. This time the context was history itself.

Only a few months before, a new President of the United States had actually uttered aloud the words "gay and lesbian" for the very first time and had, at great political cost to himself, declared his belief that we were citizens, human beings, worthy of military status (in other words, human dignity and rights). If he never did another thing, the fact that he did that for us was an incredible, costly gift. So when this funeral director said those words at the funeral of a black gay veteran, it all just came together. We just wept as he said, "On behalf of the President"—the President, Bill Clinton, someone who could at least say the words "gay and lesbian." "A grateful nation." Imagine. The United States expressing its gratitude for *our* Thomas.

Comparisons of oppression are at times very odious to me. But the feeling in that room reminded me of the feelings I saw in another room just weeks later, at the conclusion of the federal trial of the four officers accused of violating the civil rights of Rodney King. This was a national trauma, but a real local crisis and trauma in Los Angeles. The picture of the sanctuary of First AME Church in Los Angeles comes to mind, and the tears of relief and joy as the officers were finally being convicted of something. I remember Jesse Jackson wiping his own tears, saying, "Why do we have to go through all this drama to get simple justice?" Nothing in that whole day touched me more than that comment, of joy and bitterness commingled. One battle was more or less resolved, but all the problems remain, the war goes on.

All this drama for some simple justice. Just to be considered human, worthy of citizenship, worthy of heaven. For all the differences in our oppression that cannot be compared, African Americans and gay and lesbian people share this experience

When I say I'm a queer millennialist, it has to do with the justice in *heaven and on earth* stuff. In times of slavery and its aftermath, the question about black people's souls, about that dimension of their humanness, was a *de*humanizing topic of discussion. But eventually it almost seemed as if heaven, for blacks, and in fact for all poor people, was often viewed as a consolation prize for having no justice on earth.

For gays and lesbians, it's a little different. Being able to be closeted means that gays and lesbians have been able to pass and use race, gender or class privilege, where possible, to get the goodies here on earth. In fact, there is a growing stereotype, very much encouraged by the gay and lesbian political establishment, that gays and lesbians are a white, wealthy minority who can push our agenda. Well, I know a lot of poor, working-class, and nonwhite gays and lesbians. Lesbians are disproportionately represented in every women's prison I've ever visited, and these were not lesbians who were only lesbian during their prison sentence.

But the issue of heaven has been really touchy for gays and lesbians. It's the "Jack Benny thing." So I make it my practice to talk about heaven casually, freely, and frequently, as if, with Emily Dickinson, "the chart was given," like I am familiar with "the spot," and of course we're all going to get there.[1] *And I won't go without you.*

Once, while debating Jerry Falwell on Ron Reagan Jr.'s television show, I got to deliver one of my favorite "gays goin' to heaven" sound bytes. I said, "Jerry, the only reason I would want to die before you is that I want to be on heaven's welcome wagon and see the look on your face when you get there." He actually chuckled, turned to me at the break, and said, "That was very good!"

When the National Council of Churches of Christ voted in the fall of 1992 to take no action on our request for observer status (as if that in itself were not an action!), I managed to be able to say how grateful I was for UFMCC because it was there that I learned that, thank God, "it was easier to get into heaven than into the National Council of Churches of Christ in the U.S.A.!" That little *sound byte* made it to newspapers in Holland, Hong Kong and around the world. I liked saying it because it assumes that gay and lesbian people are eligible for heaven. That assumption is contained in the grammar of the sentence. And when I speak about God or heaven, I always want gay men and lesbians to hear the assumption of our eligibility (for heaven, if not for the NCC).

### The Wounds of False Witness

What are the wounds of our people the gay and lesbian, bisexual, transgender communities and tribes?

Clearly, rejection and abandonment are at the top of the list. Rejection and abandonment by our families, churches, synagogues, governments. But also high on the list for me is the damage caused by slander. There is no explicit condemnation of homosexuality among the Ten Commandments in the Bible, but there is a commandment against bearing false witness against your neighbor. Virginia Mollenkott and Letha

Our Tribe

Scanzoni wrote a book many years ago with the wonderful title *Is the Homosexual My Neighbor?* If the answer to that rhetorical question is yes, then the assumption must be that gay and lesbian people are human, are our neighbors, and that it displeases God if we tell lies about them! The Bible doesn't seem to say whether it's worse if the lies are told out of malice or ignorance. False witness is false witness.

The fact is that the *radical* or *religious* right breaks the Ninth Commandment (that prohibits false witness) every day, using ignorance and fear of homosexuality and homosexuals to raise millions and millions of dollars. But they are not alone. The whole Church and other religious bodies have borne false witness about gays and lesbians for at least a millennium.

One of the most painful false negative stereotypes about gay and lesbian people is that we are child molesters. For many, many years, police statistics have demonstrated that the vast majority (over 90 percent) of child molesters are heterosexual men. There is no factual basis whatsoever for the belief that gay men or lesbians are any more likely than heterosexuals to seduce or molest children or adolescents. Yet this fear and false witness are kept alive in the popular mind. It is one of the underlying discomforts many people have about gays in the military: parents whose children in their late teens or early 20's are joining the military fear that they will be corrupted by predatory homosexuals.

This false witness has increased the stigmatizing of homosexuality and is one of several factors that brings homophobia to the irrational, fevered pitch we experience. But even more important and tragic, gays and lesbians have our own internalized response to this stigma. One of our responses has been to be afraid of children and of interacting with them to avoid any possible cause for the accusation of child molestation. This has come out as a thinly veiled hostility toward children. I remember particularly in the '70s When we called straight people "hets" or "breeders" and the children were "rug rats" or "curtain climbers." There was the occasional lesbian mother who still had custody of her children, and a very rare father or two. But children did not often get a warm reception at gay and lesbian gatherings in those days, and in some places today, they still do not. Over time, many gays and lesbians had less contact with their own children, their nieces and nephews or with children in general. In a kind of defensive maneuver, gay men and some lesbians insulated themselves from children and from this potential slander.

This is not helped by the fact that we live in a culture that is less and less hospitable to children, and that tolerates abuse of children and record levels of poverty among children. That poverty results in more and more children not getting health care, and being chronically malnourished during the crucial years of growth and development. Ironically, gay and lesbians are disproportionately represented in the helping professionals, including teaching and healthcare, and play critical roles in shoring up the dwindling services available for children, while often being afraid to be around children in their private lives.

Underneath that defensive posture towards children has always lurked the deep-seated fear, "What if they are right?" Are children really safe with us? When I became the Pastor of MCC Detroit in 1975, the church had a *policy* that no one under the age of 18 could attend MCC without being accompanied by a parent or guardian. I was stunned that a church would feel it was too risky to welcome unaccompanied minors. This was both a fear of the false accusations that could be made *and* a deep-seated, perhaps unconscious uneasiness that maybe children weren't really safe with us. That was simply internalized homophobia. I told them I would not pastor a church where children were not safe or welcome. And in any case, we couldn't keep them away. The children managed to find us on their own.

Roger was 13 when he came to MCC Detroit. He knew he was gay, and he was very mature-appearing for his age, as well as sexually precocious. He often managed to get into gay bars and was constantly harassed at school. He was working "the block" (every city has a gay cruising area where closeted gay or bisexual men pick up hustlers or street kids for quick sex). A very closeted member of my church picked Roger up, then realized how old he was. The member called me in a panic. He brought Roger to me at the church office and dropped him off.

I called his mother. She couldn't handle him, couldn't keep him in school, so I offered to help. I got written permission from her for him to attend the church (to ease the minds of Board members, so that she couldn't later accuse us of welcoming Roger without her knowledge or consent). Two adult men in the church took Roger under their wing. These were two men who did not exploit him sexually but gave him support and sometimes even shelter. They did this at great risk to themselves. We managed to help get Roger safely through junior high, and he eventually moved to San Francisco to complete high school.

51

Metropolitan Community Church of Los Angeles tells the story of a young boy (not older than 12), a runaway, who appeared on the steps of the church on a Sunday in the early '70s. He wanted to go home. So the assistant pastor took him to the police. It is hard for anyone who is not gay or lesbian and over 35 to understand what an enormous act of courage this was on the part of the pastor. The pastor explained what had happened, and the police spent time interrogating the boy, trying to find out, among other things, if these homosexuals had molested him in any way. Finally, one of the officers said, "Son, do you know what kind of church this is?" and the boy thought for a minute and replied, "I don't know, I guess it's just a church for everybody." That story has been told a lot at MCC L.A. It contains a lot of healing messages.

UFMCC says we are a church for everybody—including children. In the 1980s, two things happened, it almost seems simultaneously: the AIDS epidemic (which began devastating the gay male community especially) and the lesbian (and to a lesser extent, gay male) baby boom. More lesbians and gay men were fighting for the right to have full or partial custody of their children from heterosexual marriages or relationships. And lesbians were seeking other ways to have children, especially through artificial insemination and adoption. Some gay men also donated sperm or sought to adopt.

Many MCC churches now have child care or children's programs. But there is still resistance to this in the gay and lesbian community—remnants of the negative power of false witness.

I have come to believe that our capacity to welcome children into our gay and lesbian families, organizations, churches and so on is one measure of how much healing we have experienced. Our resistance to children is our resistance to own healing. The safer children are with us, the safer we are with ourselves and each other.

This is also related to the relatively new "inner-child" psychology. When we welcome real live children into our communities or churches, we also have to face our own wounded inner child. More often than not, our gay or lesbian inner child was rejected, abandoned or abused. I believe that oftentimes our families knew before we did that we were gay or lesbian. At least that we were different. They may not have known why. But we were different, some of us "passing" for straight better than others. And that difference was not perceived as a good thing. It caused us to be punished, humiliated, targeted for abuse.

It has not been easy for gay men and lesbians to admit these childhood wounds, partly because of another false witness. That one said that we became gay or lesbian because of an "absent father" and an "overbearing mother"; or because we were molested by an older homosexual (and then wanted to grow up and be one?); or molested heterosexually (and we hated it and wanted not to be one of them?).

One old gay expression used to be that one "turned" gay like milk that was "turning" sour! In any case, to admit to having been targeted for emotional or physical abuse seemed to be contributing to a negative stereotype! So many of us were anxious, in fact, overanxious to prove that we came from "normal" homes and parents, which most of us did. Except that today, we know that "normal homes and parents" in America are often very violent and abusive: something we did not know as well in the early days of our movement.

If you read Troy Perry's autobiographical books, separated by nearly two decades, you can see the difference in consciousness illustrated quite dramatically. In the *Lord Is My Shepherd and He Knows I'm Gay,* Troy presents a mostly happy childhood picture, glossing over some crucial issues. In *Don't Be Afraid Anymore,* he tells some terrible stories about violence and abuse in his family and childhood. It became safer and more acceptable for Troy to tell those stories in the late 1980s.

And telling those stories is what we must do if we are to heal and if we are really to be a safe haven for the children we want to welcome into our lives.

I met Rechal in October 1985. She was three years old, and I met her in prison.

She and her mother were in prison together in a special facility operated by the California Department of Corrections. This program and several others like it probably had good theory and intentions. It was a locked facility for women who had infants or toddlers. The theory was that these women and their children would benefit from not losing contact with one another during the crucial formative years. Also, the women could be given assistance in learning parenting skills.

Instead, this program, in my opinion, amounted to women in prison providing the care for these children for free, so that the state would not have to pay for their support while the mothers were in prison. It was a budgeting cutting reform masquerading as "keeping families together." There were no classes or other assistance in parenting skills. And because these women were locked up 24 hours a day, they had 24-hour sole care of the children, no breaks provided. No mothers-in-law, or sisters or other family members available to give the mothers a break. Never. And some of the children were old enough to be conscious of living in a locked facility.

Jessie was an attractive 38-year-old career criminal and the mother of Rechal. Jessie had been introduced to the Mexican equivalent of the Mafia at an early age by her family. She laundered money, did robberies. She was openly proud of the fact that she had refused to engage in prostitution and had always lived her lesbian identity, with occasionally heterosexual involvements. She had been party to a killing, something she referred to, but could never bring herself to talk about with me.

As happens with organized crime, Jessie had ended up owing someone a lot of money (she was a heroin addict). Rechal was a late-in-life baby that she desperately wanted to have, and she finally really wanted to get off drugs and out of the organized crime scene. So she agreed to assist in one *last* diamond heist to pay off her debt. She was arrested, and Rechal was taken from her.

While in prison, Jessie heard of UFMCC. When she got released to this special facility, she contacted me at UFMCC's headquarters. She had called other gay and lesbian organizations looking for support or help, to no avail. MCC Los Angeles had just begun an outreach program at California Institute for Women, and Jessie's lover, Carol, gave her our phone number.

Jessie was shocked when someone actually called her back. She was looking for legal assistance for her other 12-year-old developmentally-disabled daughter who was being held in the Juvenile Hall. I got a referral for her and then asked her if she wanted me to come visit her. She was cautious but said yes. A few days later I showed up, wearing my clerical collar, at the facility (which was temporarily housed in one wing of a rehab center in South Central Los Angeles).

After I cleared security, they let me in the locked ward. Jessie and Rechal greeted me.

I picked up three-year-old Rechal and fell in love at first sight She sat on my lap, pointed to my collar, and said, "Jesus?" Then she asked me if I was a boy or a girl (Rechal had only been to Catholic churches at this point in her life). After we established my true name and gender, I got to know them both over several months.

Jessie asked me to baptize Rechal and to become her godmother. It was clear that Jessie had few friends and resources that she could count on, and her family was simply not an option. Jessie began testing me. Was I reliable? In retrospect, I know she was trying to determine if her child would be safe with me.

After knowing them a few months, Jessie asked me to take care of Rechal while she had minor surgery—for four or five days. This was another test from Jessie. I agreed to take Rechal. For all their locked wards and security, they just let me sign this three year old out. They asked for no identification. I could have taken her then and never returned. It overwhelmed me—how unimportant Rechal's life was to this institution. But how important to her mother.

I did bring Rechal home, after talking it over with Paula. However, Jessie was not well after returning back to prison from surgery. In fact, she had a high fever, and perhaps an infection. She called me, apologetic, desperate, very, very ill. They would not take her to the hospital. She cried, saying, "I'm so sorry to call you—but I have no one else." I called the prison, to no avail. Finally, in the middle of the night, I drove to the facility, pounded on the door, and made them talk to me, and told them to get her to a hospital or all hell would break loose.

They called her a cab and accompanied her, and she took three more weeks to recover, having come very close to dying. I returned Rechal to the facility with her mother, and we had to make plans for their release. I helped find a housing situation for Jessie and Rechal with the plan that they would receive support and help from the MCC community.

It seemed ideal. My friend Judi had an adopted son and a large home. We worked on the finances, the roommate arrangement, and I began talking with Jessie about what she really wanted in her life. She was a jazz pianist, and she was going to play in church sometime soon. She had been off drugs since before Rechal was born. It seemed very hopeful to me.

After nearly a week, I had a sobering conversation with Jessie, in which she seemed agitated and restless, not happy with the arrangements, and very down on herself, and her ability to "make it," to really pull her life together, to provide a home for Rechal. I was very worried when I left her that day, overwhelmed by Jessie's despair. Later that day, she died of a heroin overdose in the bathroom of my friend's home. Rechal was with her for four hours, curled up beside her, before Judi and her son came home and found them.

The next week was a nightmare of waiting to find out about Rechal's whereabouts. The police had taken her into protective custody and would not let me take her home with me (unlike the last time when no one cared who took Rechal home with them.) I understood that in the chaos of those hours, with a dead woman on the bathroom floor, they had no way to verify whether or not the rest of us were involved in drug abuse.

Judi and I spent days talking about what was best for Rechal. Judi had a lot of experience with children who had been traumatized. We came to the conclusion that if Judi could adopt her, I could continue to be in Rechal's life as an "extra mommy" that is, godmother.

Miraculously, in March of 1986, an L.A. court agreed. When Rechal's grandmother decided to try to get involved, an independent, court-appointed guardian investigated. It was Rechal's grandmother, Jessie's own mother, who had gotten Jessie involved in organized crime and probably with drugs, in the first place. The court believed us, and Rechal found a home and a wonderful, large family that now includes other abandoned, endangered children.

Rechal is an incredible blessing in my life. She has continued to have struggles of her own as she has grown into a young woman. She is one of thousands and thousands of children who have been lucky enough to find safe, loving, gay and lesbian homes to live in.

Gay men and lesbians were among the first people to offer foster care and adoption to children with HIV and AIDS. When others were afraid or turned off, gay men and lesbians, who already had had lots of contact with people with AIDS, were not afraid to touch or love these children. Lesbians founded most of the agencies that service children with HIV and AIDS. The wounds from the false witness of Church and society against us will take a long time to heal, especially the insinuation that we are gay or lesbian because of a poor upbringing and that we are all consequently child molesters. Only telling the stories of the healing of our own families of origin from this false witness, and the creation of our own families of choice (which often include children) will begin to heal these wounds completely.

## The Wounds from Projection and Repression

I think the other way in which gay and lesbian people and other sexual minorities experience oppression is that we have endured the massive projection of society's sexual fears and fantasies.

Most minorities experience sexual projection as part of their oppression. African-Americans, male and female, experience sexual projection as part of the package of white racism. African-American men have been stereotyped as sexually obsessed and violent (there is, for example, the "myth of the black rapist"),[2] and African-American women have been stereotyped as promiscuous. Asian-Americans are considered sexually exotic by the white majority, and Latins are supposed to be "hot." And of course, sexism's major features include the projection of male fears and fantasies onto women so that women are not real people but objects available for male sexual pleasure or objects over which men can exercise power and control.

If racial and ethnic minorities are the objects of sexual projection, how much more is this true for sexual minorities where the issue of sexuality is already at the forefront of the collective consciousness.

Society's hatred and loathing of homosexuals is really about the collective shame, guilt, fear, and self-hatred in our culture at large, especially as these are related to issues of sexuality.

*Presbyterians and Human Sexuality*, published by the Special Committee on Human Sexuality of the Presbyterian Church in the United States, said this: "The special committee noticed how the problem of homosexuality is commonly used in our churches to refer indirectly to any and all forms of sexual nonconformity, whether among gay persons or non-gays. Homosexuality is typically invoked in a rhetorical, almost formulaic way to signal that something has gone wrong. However, homosexuality often remains an abstraction, unrelated to—and uninformed by—real people. It functions primarily as a powerful symbolic carrier of people's fears and discomfort about sexuality in general."[3]

I'm tempted to say here, "We knew that!" Gay and lesbian people, however, do and do not know this. Sometimes it comes out in the kind of campy, teasing, "gotcha" gay-pride rhetoric: "Two, four, six, eight, is your husband really straight?" "We are your worst fears and your best fantasies." "We are the people your mother warned you about." And so on!

At other times we gays and lesbians are ourselves bewildered. In many ways we are symbolic of the current struggle over changing sexual roles that is going on in many cultures. That struggle is occurring in the context of a global women's movement that seeks to expose and bring about the end of patriarchy. No wonder there is lots of fear and projection going on.

If Judy Grahn is correct in her theory that gays, lesbians, and transpeople function to explore the future for the culture, then it is possible that society will project its fears about the future (especially its fears about gender and sexuality) onto us.

I never feel as queer at home or at MCC Los Angeles as I do when I am in a predominantly heterosexual setting, like at the NCC meetings. Just by showing up, we trigger people's questions, fears, anxieties and fantasies about homosexuality or sexuality in general. This is exhausting. And yet, it feels like it is part of my job, our job, to invite questions, speculations, *even* their projections. But I find myself wanting to retreat to the safety of the gay/lesbian "ghetto."

I had a interesting experience while on vacation, recently, with Paula in northern California. We were visiting Paula's best friend, Suzanne, and her husband Ed. Suzanne's brother and his new wife stopped by one evening, and our pre-dinner conversation fell to talking about families, functional and otherwise, and marriage. Both these couples are sophisticated and accepting, but we all had a moment of slight surprise when we realized that Paula and I had the longest-lasting marriage. Suzanne quipped that she had been married as long as Paula and I, but to three different men! The same was roughly true for the other couple. Paula then piped up about the Pete Knight referendum (Proposition 22) in California that would oppose anything but heterosexual marriage. Suzanne's sister-in-law spoke up and said well, she thought it was fine for gay people to get married, but just as long as we are ready to have the responsibilities and deal with divorce, etc. Now, I know she was just reflecting on her own difficulties, and perhaps envious of her fantasies of "responsibility immune" homosexuals. But it felt so condescending and so strange to have to continue to educate people, even very supportive people, in a this relatively benign, social setting.

When I think of all the gay men and lesbians, who without the benefit or "responsibilities" of legal marriage, care for dying partners, handle financial, legal and other issues with grace and love and compassion, I am amazed that anyone can think we don't know about "responsibility."

I think of how many lesbians and gay men raise each other's children and grandchildren, care for each other's parents, stand by one another "for better, for worse, for richer for poorer, in sickness and in health, 'til death do us part," it amazes me. Don't lecture me about responsibilities! We've had plenty, and without protection or support from the culture at large, the government, or, often, our families or religious institutions. Not that everyone in our community is always a model of perfect commitment. Every community has its flakes and deadbeats, its exploiters and sociopaths. But we certainly don't have more than our share.

It is one thing to experience the sometimes amusing/sometimes insulting projections of ordinary everyday garden variety homophobia. It is still another thing to be the projection of the church's or society's fears to the degree that one is labeled evil or demonic. This is another experience that ordinary gay and lesbian people have—some frequently, some from time to time. I know many gays and lesbians who have been forbidden to have any contact with their own or their siblings' children because of the assumed "toxicity" of their presence or influence. Or other gays and lesbians who have been publicly outed, humiliated, vilified, and literally driven out of a church meeting or Bible study, or pastor's office, or confessional. Many gay and lesbian individuals do not have the resources internally to cope with these experiences. Some do not understand that this is a result of homophobia. They really believe they must deserve it, even if they can't figure out why.

Sandy Taylor came to my office one day in Detroit, Michigan, having received our church newsletter in the mail, and, noting that there was a new woman pastor at MCC, decided to check me out. Sandy was a petite, attractive, social worker in her late 20's. She had a spiritual chip on her shoulder, and a look in her eyes that made me know she had once loved God, and really missed having a spiritual life. I feel privileged to have become part of her life and to be part of her ministry.

It took several years before I learned the whole story. She was raised Baptist, in a small city in Ohio. From the time she was little, a next door neighbor, grandmother like figure, told her stories of Jesus that comforted and fascinated her. But when Sandy was only eight years old, her grandfather began molesting her. At age ten, she became pregnant, without even knowing or understanding what was happening to her. She was given a back street abortion and nearly died.

No one in her family, to Sandy's knowledge, ever confronted her grandfather. Even after this terrible experience, he was still permitted to come to her house (though she was never alone with him again). He would be invited to Sunday dinner every week. Sandy had a powerful, strong spirit that somehow had not been crushed. She informed her parents that if they were going to continue to invite him to Sunday dinner, she would just excuse herself and not be present. She ate no Sunday dinner the rest of the years she lived at home. It was her dignified, silent, but visible protest.

Later, she would marry, and attend Mid-Western Bible College in Michigan. There, she found herself attracted to another woman, without even really understanding the nature of that attraction, and certainly without having any overt sexual contact. Her marriage was deteriorating, and the school decided that this was Sandy's fault. One day they publicly excoriated her in the chapel, during a service. She left the school, divorced Gary and became a social worker.

Sandy eventually left social work to become an MCC minister. She was able to reclaim her Baptist roots, heal from the fundamentalism and pain, for the most part, forgive God. She never completely healed from the psychological wounds of incest and religious persecution, however. Only a few years into her ministry, she began a protracted struggle with breast cancer. She spent the rest of her too-short life helping others recovering from incest and abuse, physical, mental and spiritual, done to them in the name of God, and under cover of family secrets. In 1983 she died of an apparent overdose of Tylenol.

The other wound related to projection is that of repression. We become obsessed with what we repress. Our culture has historically been sexually repressive and has become sexually obsessive. The gay and lesbian movement is both a consequence of and a contributor to this progression from repression to obsession. If society has repressed homosexuals and homosexuality, then it is also likely to become obsessed with it. Just think of how often gays and lesbians have been the subject of talk shows over the last 15 years or so. Talking about homosexuality almost assures a good audience. Televangelists know that by talking about us on television or in their fund-raising mail they will get a lot of attention and response. If both repression and obsession are unhealthy and damaging responses to the gift of human sexuality, than what should be happening?

Gift. That's the key, I think. Sexuality is a part of our humanness that needs to be accepted, nurtured, and valued as a gift.

Meanwhile, however, homosexuality does not feel like a gift to the dominant culture! It represents all the "bad" things that sex is: dirty, promiscuous, shameful, perverted, weird, unhealthy, predatory, bad for children, nonproductive.

Many heterosexual people imagine that gay sexuality feels perverted, weird and slimy, even to us! As gay and lesbian children grow up, we learn, overtly or indirectly, how dirty and awful "it" is. Then comes the conflicting thoughts, feelings, longings, desires. How can I want to touch and be touched in a way that feels "bad" or that God and everyone else will hate?

I remember first knowing that there were gay men when I was in junior high school. The limited information I had was that they all lived in Greenwich Village, New York, or on Fire Island (off of Long Island, where I lived). They were men who wore dresses and acted effeminate, I thought. It was years before I knew that they actually had sex with each other, and I learned the words "queer" and "lezzie." (A favorite junior high slogan, as I recall was, "lez-be queer and go homo!").

A "lezzie" was a tomboy who forgot to grow out of it. I was a tomboy who was making a valiant effort to grow out of it. Lezzies wanted to be boys. I may have even known that lezzies wanted to touch other girls the ways boys were supposed to want to touch girls. Actually, I didn't know very much about that either, come to think of it.

I knew the essentials about the mechanics of heterosexual intercourse. But my mother told me that you were only supposed to do this when you were married. She blushed when she told me. And she told me it was enjoyable. I remember having serious doubts about that at the time. I knew that my parents hugged and kissed—I saw them do it. And they certainly liked it. I liked being hugged and kissed. So they hugged and kissed, and then, at some opportune moment, he stuck his penis into her vagina. I did not even understand this as a process, only as an event! I did not understand lovemaking as an activity that would take some time.

Only gradually, I suppose, as I saw peers "making out" or as movies became a little more graphic did I understand anything about heterosexual sexual arousal. So it was all very strange and mysterious. I was in seminary and 21 years old before I ever recall seeing an erect penis. It was an 80-year-old disabled priest's in the hospital where I worked. (He was on

61

a powerful drug whose side effect was sexual arousal.) Every other penis I'd seen had been flaccid. Only then did I actually under stand how the penis got into the vagina.

I do remember the night that my friend Jean came over to the house where I was baby-sitting. Jean was moving to Connecticut. I was almost 15, she was 14. It broke my heart to have to say good-bye. She walked over early one evening, and we knew that her grandfather was going to come get her in half an hour. I had put the babies to bed. We sat on the stairway that led to the den. On an impulse that I think I understood more than I really wanted to, I put my arm around her shoulder. I longed to do that. In fact I longed to do more, although I wasn't exactly sure what. It was my first homoerotic gesture. I pulled her to me sideways, just a little, sitting next to her on the stairs. I loved Jean; I hated that she was leaving me. I wanted to touch her. I did.

Twenty-five years later Jean and I would finally talk about that moment and others like it that had shaped our adolescence. Jean told me that she had searched for pictures of the feeling she had when I had held her that night. The closest thing she had found was a classic picture of Jesus touching someone in a gesture of healing. I cried when she wrote to me about that. Jesus, touch, sexuality. Watch out, Nancy, they're going to go nuts!

The hard part for me as an adolescent was that I could not afford to know that my longing to touch Jean was about my sexuality. I think this is true of many lesbians and gay men, although it does seem that gay men, like all men in our culture, have more access to information about sexuality than do lesbians.

So I repressed my natural, developing lesbian sexual longings or compartmentalized and mislabeled them. Then I waited for the hetero-sexual desires, lust, to sort of *happen* to me. It never quite did. Not clearly. Not enough. So I kept waiting and waiting and meanwhile became a great student and a musician. I also got into religion. I kept very, very busy.

I remember going to the movies to see D. H. Lawrence's *The Fox* with the woman who would eventually become my first lover. We were probably juniors in college at the time. I had never seen a woman kiss another woman on the mouth. This film contained one scene in which a woman actually kissed another on the mouth in a prone position. I cannot describe my mixed feelings of excitement, anticipation and terror, and I remember covering my face with my hands and peaking through. Then, in an instant, it was over. No one died. I do, however, remember the noises of disgust from the audience. It really didn't look strange or awful to me. And I didn't want to think about that!

Part of healing and coming out for me was the process of "unrepressing," actually uncovering the truth about sexual feelings, touching, arousal, pleasure. Learning to find out for myself, not to take anyone else's word for it. Not even D. H. Lawrence's. Beginning, day by day, to throw off the projection, the fears. I'm still learning how to do it.

I had to learn that there is nothing particularly exotic or weird about homosexuality. I had to learn to recover from my own sexual and emotional isolation. To recognize sexual arousal, erotic impulses, and fantasies in myself. To learn how my own body likes to touch and be touched. I had a lot of remedial work to do. I had starved myself sexually, because I thought this would keep me from being punished and despised.

If sexuality is a part of life, a gift to help us be more fully alive, Jesus must have included sexuality in his promise, "I came that they may have life and have it more abundantly" (John 10:10).

After I came out, and came into UFMCC, I immediately had to deal with sexual projection. On top of being an open lesbian, I came out publicly almost immediately as a lesbian clergy, a pastor in a gay church. In the late fall of 1972, my picture appeared on the front page of the city section of the Boston Globe: instant public queer at age 22.

In about 1974, when I was pastoring MCC Worcester, Massachusetts, I got a call from someone who wanted to talk to me. We had no church office, except in my kitchen. For reasons of safety, I didn't meet strangers in my home very often, but when I did, I always made sure that my lover or another member of the church was present. For some reason, it was more convenient to have this man come talk to me in my kitchen, while Heather waited in the living room.

A mousy-looking older white man appeared at my door, looking a little anxious. He sat in my kitchen, hemmed and hawed, then began telling me about himself. He had asked me early on if I was a lesbian, and I had said yes. He then told me about a visit to a massage parlor in western Massachusetts, and over a long half hour, he told me that a woman there had given him an enema, which he had found sexually stimulating. It turned out that this was a new experience for him (and since I had never heard of such a thing, it was becoming a new experience for me!). The massage parlor had been closed down. He also thought that this woman was a lesbian. Sooo, finally he got around to asking me, if, since I was a lesbian, would I be willing to give him an enema?

Well, no one at Boston University School of Theology had prepared me for this type of pastoral counseling inquiry. I continued to manage my facial expression while clearly and firmly telling him that I would not be willing to give him an enema. Also, that I was afraid that he did not have a very good understanding of what a lesbian was and that I was the pastor of a church. You know, a place where people sat in pews (or in our case, on folding chairs), and sang hymns, listened to a sermon, took communion, and went home. No enemas.

Actually, I was neither sarcastic or unkind. I felt sorry for him because he did not quite know how to get his needs met. On some level of human connection, I certainly understood. I had spent many years hiding from my own sexuality, with many people still think is weird or strange. Who was I to judge him? I told him to ask for help at a particular notorious bookstore in town that might have "referrals." (I bet the local Lutheran pastor would not have been able to handle it that way!)

It did shake me up just a bit, though, to think of the many fantastic and unusual ways in which people viewed me (and other UFMCC or gay and lesbian clergy). In some ways, I feel like I am a modest, rather conventional person in my sexual needs and expression. In the '70s, especially, UFMCC clergy were often the only openly gay people in their city or town. This is still true in the more rural areas of the United States and in other countries. We had to know more than we might have wanted to know about lots of different sexualities, including (as I found out) information about enemas, sex toys, and bookstores, pornography, S&M, transvestism, leather and lace, transsexualism, bisexuality. We spoke at colleges and health classes about our sexuality. We had to learn to speak publicly and comfortably about male and female anatomy and sex practices and how to handle homophobic, ignorant, hostile questions and comments. Over and over and over, we were taught as UFMCC clergy such things as how to put our books about sexuality at eye level in our offices so that parishioners would feel comfortable enough to talk with us about their sexuality. We were to model healthy and open attitudes about sexuality in our words and behavior.

Our parishioners did talk to us about sexuality a lot. We helped them come out, helped them talk about relationships, dating, sexual hang-ups, guilt and fear. It was a kind of on-the-job training: everything you wanted to know and more. Sometimes much more!

And many gay people hadn't learned or quite internalized the vocabulary. My friend Phil, never very good at correct word choices used to say he had a "monotonous" (meaning monogamous) relationship with his boyfriend. I remember counselling two young guys for a Holy Union, and when I asked them if they were "monogamous' the one fellow piped up, "Oh, no pastor, sometimes he does the dishes, and sometimes I do!"

Then there was the very, very effeminate young man, Caesar, who was still learning English. He came to me, deeply troubled because he was afraid that he was "bisexual." I was quite curious about this, and, frankly, looking at him, incredulous. "What do you mean, bisexual?" Well, words alone apparently couldn't express what he was trying to communicate. With a mixture of hand gestures and words he managed to tell me that in his last relationship he had been the "bottom," the more "passive" partner, and in his new relationship (also with a man), he was the "top," or the more active partner. He thought that was "bisexual." It always helps to ask.

We, MCC clergy and lay leaders, have had to try to help others heal and be comfortable with their sexuality while we were still discovering ours. It's amazing that people survived our early efforts.

I discovered that people are sometimes curious about the sex lives of clergy, including gay and lesbian clergy. Sometimes people have assumed that I'm celibate (they think I'm a nun). This has been true for heterosexual Christian clergy as well. Troy used to say that when he was in the Church of God of Prophecy, heterosexual male members of his church would boast and hand out cigars when they had fathered a child. When a clergyman fathered a child, however, it was sort of a big secret. The child was a gift from God, as if sex had nothing to do with it.

Sometimes I am surprised by how easy it is for some people to talk about their sex lives and how difficult it is for others. For some people it is a lot harder and even more intimate to talk about their spiritual lives than it is to talk about their sex lives.

People also have incredible psychological transference issues with clergy, something I never learned about in seminary. And it's even more complex when you are a clergyperson in a sexual minority community. We are only beginning to know how powerful the role of a clergyperson is in our culture. My experience is that many people project onto me their fears and wishes about God, which makes the issue of transference even more complex.

On top of that, clergy have overlapping relationships structured into our lives. The same people with whom we serve on the church board, and with whom we may have a difference of opinion, may be the same board member who has to call us later that night with news of a family tragedy or some other personal issue. We socialize at church events, hear confessions, do marriage counselling with people we may later have to ask for a donation for the building fund.

Some parishioners never call me by my first name, others always do. Some I can speak with quite personally. Other avoid that, because it is too much information about someone they hold in high esteem or about whom they make certain, and often incorrect, assumptions. Some people apologize, deeply and seriously, if they use a swear word in my presence. One woman came into the church on a Saturday, when I was cleaning my office and doing filing, wearing my blue jeans, and she said, "O my God, I've never seen you without your clothes on!" (meaning my church vestments). When she realized what she said, she was mortified. At a church beach party some members were shocked to see me boogie boarding. To think of me at play, a nearly 50 year old lesbian doing what kids like to do was somehow surprising, and the topic of conversation, I later learned.

The truth is, for some people, boogie boarding isn't a very spiritual activity, and those vestments are my clothes—seeing me in blue jeans or a bathing suit just blows the image thing all to hell! Other people are thrilled and happy to have a pastor who is a real person, and can tolerate church a lot more because I am all too obviously human most of the time!

I think people feel awkward and may experience transference to one degree or another with all clergy. I remember how hard it was for my mother to call the assistant pastor of the church we attended by his first name. He was her age and a kind, committed pastor. But clergy had this aura, this mystique. They weren't quite human in a relaxed sort of way, and maybe we didn't want them to be. We certainly didn't want to particularly think of them as sexual beings (but since he had five children, it was a little hard to avoid.). But, it is even more complicated when you are the pastor of a church that ministers to a sexual minority.

Because clergy are authority figures, they sometimes abuse that authority. Some clergy also have a lot of difficulty managing the role. We think we're supposed to be perfect, have perfect families, never have doubts or weaknesses. Then we become hopelessly neurotic and wonder why! Or we become clergy because we're already that way!

People come to my office saying they are afraid of me and don't know why. Usually it's because they were afraid of a clergyperson from early in their life, or more probably, they are afraid of God. Or they fall in love with me, as they are falling in love with God. If they hate God, they sometimes hate me—after all, they can *see* me!

I have had to learn ways to hold up a mirror and help people see that their feelings about me tell them about themselves. Mostly, thankfully, the transference really has nothing to do with me! But, if I am needy or vulnerable, I may forget that fact. One mentally disturbed woman at MCC L.A. would follow me around after services cursing and saying horrible, cruel things to me. I knew she was a wounded child of God, but there were times I just wanted her to disappear!

I meet women and men all the time who were molested or abused by clergy or church leaders, some of whom were their parents or relatives. It is extremely hard for them to think that they can ever trust a religious authority figure again. One young man came to my office very upset, saying that he knew this was probably not true, but he thought that I had told him never to come back to the church during my sermon the Sunday before. He was very agitated and obviously frightened to be in my office. I assumed that for him to have this powerful an experience, something must have happened to him earlier in his life. After assuring him that I had not said that to him or anyone during the service, he told me that he had lived in a foster home as a child with a pastor who sexually molested him for years. He had no trust of clergy, and was very conflicted about even coming to a church. It was a miracle that he even had the courage to come to church or my office. He cried, we prayed, and met a couple of times, until he felt safer in my presence and in the church.

In many ancient cultures, gays and lesbians were not the objects of sexual projection, at least not in a negative sense. Native Americans call us the "two-spirited people," meaning that we have both male and female spirits. Gays and lesbians were often seen as specifically blessed, not specifically cursed, as it were, "double" people rather than "half a man" or "half a woman."

So, how are we (modern gay men and lesbians and other sexual minorities) to see ourselves? As broken or as gifted? As both? As wounded healers of our culture's sexual repression-obsession polarity?

Gay men and lesbians are in a sense forced to work on our sexual healing just to survive in a homophobic culture. The world needs to know what we have been learning while we have been healing. Because what have learned together and who we've become as we've learned it are the source of tribal gifts we long to offer to the world.

# Chapter Two—Boldly Exercising Our Tribal Gifts

It is an audacious thing, this time of millennial shift, to claim purpose and meaning for gay and lesbian people on the planet. How unbelievable to claim that those who were labeled sick, perverted, criminals and the *foulest* of sinners could have personal, cultural, spiritual, yes, tribal gifts to share!

Part of moving beyond, way beyond apologetics is to assert that we are not an aberration. We are not a deformity, a mistake. We are not a genetic deficiency that needs to be tolerated or eradicated. We are not an annoying group of sex fiends seeking to legitimize perverted sex in the streets or the schoolyards.

We are a necessary part of creation, biologically, sociologically, spiritually. We, like others—not more or less than others—contribute to the wholeness, the multidimensionality of creation. *Neither creation nor the Church is complete without us.*

Just to prove this point, some of us have had fantasies for years about what it would be like if all gay, lesbian, and transpeople were suddenly visible one day, if we all turned purple at once, and could not hide what a large minority we are. Or if we all just had a massive walkout one day. Now, when I claim that we have tribal gifts, it is not accurate or necessary to say that all gay and lesbian people have these gifts in equal measure or will necessarily choose to exercise them. But we seem to bear them together.

### Gift Number 1   Coming Out

First we offer the gift of coming out. The expression "to come out" is now used generically. It has already been co-opted by the dominant culture. It simply means to tell the truth, to disclose the hitherto private, hidden realities of our lives. People come out of the closet about all kinds of things these days, and sexuality is only one of them.

We gay and lesbian people were told we'd better lie to survive. But lying about our sexuality made us sick and afraid. And sometimes it inured us to the act of lying itself.

I remember that in the bar culture of my early coming-out days, many people had aliases or nicknames. You just assumed you probably didn't know people's real names or where they really worked or the real story of their lives. One had to suspend judgment, not ask too many questions, and not get caught believing too many lies. For some, lying became positively an art form, almost as if in requiring us to lie, the world didn't deserve the truth from us. Sometimes, in sad surreal ways, there was more truth in our lying than in the facts that passed for truth. Before the days when sobriety began to heal us, we hardly even held each other accountable for the lying. A lot of it was harmless, any way, or so we thought. However, we really didn't like ourselves when we were liars. So we've stopped lying. And we've paid dearly for the privilege of telling the truth. The truth is costly sometimes. But it is worth it. I'm not sure if I have ever met anyone who has ultimately regretted coming out, no matter what price he or she paid. That excludes, of course, those who died telling the truth about their sexuality.

Gays and lesbians can take courage in Jesus' words, "you shall know the truth, and the truth shall make you free" (John 8:32). Now, I know that he meant the truth about himself and who he was and is. But he said the truth. As if all truth is connected. Like there aren't different kinds of truth. That every truth is connected to and somehow supports every other truth. To follow Christ is to live in the truth, the whole truth. When the Church, or an group or community, tells people that their participation depends on their willingness to lie about who they are, that is degrading and un-Christlike.

I have to confess that I have never understood people who went to seminary, got ordained, and pastored church while lying about their sexuality. I'm not only talking about not mentioning it, or hiding it from view

70

but also blatantly denying it and lying about it. Such people deceive them-selves into believing that this is "working for acceptance for gays and lesbians from within." From within what? From within a system of lies, which rewards lying and liars? My bias is that if you're not ready to come out, don't lie to get into seminary, to get ordained, or to get a job in a church. Wait until you can tell the truth and pay the price.

Now, I know there are people who disagree, some of them friends of mine, Catholic priests who live with their lovers and think no one knows. There are Bishops who reward people who tow the party line while re-maining closeted; and women in high places in respectable denomina-tions who can't be seen with me publicly. At some level, I can't help believe it is soul-killing. Because lying is soul killing. Jesus did not ask us to lie in order to serve him, or God, or the Church. Stop lying to your-self and the world. Stop disrespecting your relationships and friendships. It is the squandering of one of our most treasured tribal gifts: telling the truth, coming out when it is costly and can make a difference.

Why is it so hard to tell the truth in the Church? I was present for the NCC general board meeting at which Marie Fortune made a presentation on issues of domestic violence in the context of the Church. I watched the audience shut down, as if to say, "No, no, no, don't force us to hear this." The Church does not want to hear the truth about its own complicity in violence—toward children, toward women, toward gays and lesbians or anyone else.

M. Scott Peck, in *People of the Lie*[1] did a lot to help me understand the connection between psychology and spirituality in the *diagnosis* of human evil. Peck says that the connection between lying and evil is a complex and profound one. When anyone asks or encourages someone to lie, they expose them to the *tools* of evil. In a sense, the truth is our spiri-tual equivalent of an immune system. To lie, to encourage lying as a strat-egy for handling problems, is to compromise our spiritual health. What might the connection be between diseases of the physical immune sys-tem and political and psychological oppression, including the rewarding of lying?

Conversely, to tell the truth is to increase our spiritual health. There is a saying in the therapeutic community: "We are only as sick as our secrets." I believe this is why gay and lesbian people need to tell their coming-out stories over and over again. After all the fear, lying, and hid-ing, telling the truth is positively sacramental. It is a rite of purification.

Gay and lesbian people need to bathe and bask in the truth. I think I am most angry about the way in which homophobia at its core has exposed my people to the spiritual dis-ease of lies and lying. We are those who have suffered the oppression not so much perhaps of compulsory heterosexuality but of compulsive lying. The truth is making us free, and becoming truth tellers is a great gift we bring. Any state, church, institution, or individual who encourages gays, lesbians, or bisexuals to lie in order to survive (or to "succeed") contributes to the vulnerability of our people to disease and spiritual or psychological sickness.

Telling the truth literally raised our communities from the dead, and helped prepare us for dealing with death in healthier ways.

### Gift Number 2   Same Sex Eroticism

Harry Hay calls homosexuality *subject-subject sexuality*[2]—that is, as opposed to *subject-object sexuality*. Now, the truth is that gay and lesbian people are just as capable as anyone of sexually objectifying another. An there are heterosexuals who in spite of patriarchy, manage relationships that are not objectifying. However, it is also true that sex in the Western patriarchal model has more often than not been about the eroticization of dominance and dependency. In a culture where men and women are no equal politically, most heterosexual sexuality, by definition, lacks the possibility of thoroughgoing mutuality and informed consent. That's an astonishing perspective that is at the heart of the feminist critique of culture.

I remember first hearing Freda Smith's poem "Dear Dora/Dangerous Derek Diesel Dyke"[3] in the early 1970's. She spoke of the special passion of touching and being touched by one whose body is "as known as your own." Ours can be a sexuality not distorted by the politics of patriarchy to the degree that heterosexuality still must be. Even within the very gay and comparatively nonhierarchical MCC church experience, there is—and must be—"church within the church" for lesbians.

There has been something absolutely transformative about my relationships with powerful lesbian women who are taking the texts of Christianity, the sacred elements of our tradition, into our own *lesbian hands*. We are daring to uncover the connection of the erotic and the spiritual. The patriarchal, heterosexual model said that friendship was never sexy. But the eroticism of friendship is one of the wonderful tribal gifts we, as gay and lesbian people, bring.[4]

UFMCC holds regular clergy and leadership conferences in the United States to provide continuing education and mutual support. Really, though, these meetings were just an excuse to see our friends—to see the only other people in the world who were trying to make gay and lesbian church with our bare hands, no money, few resources. Except, of course, the resources of our courage and creativity. So we came to Camp Letts (YMCA) in the spring of 1982 in rural Maryland.

Partway through our several days together, someone from the YMCA noticed we were gay. The camp director with whom I had dealt with months before had moved on. The new director claimed to be totally surprised by who we really were. The camp "authorities" tried to make us leave. We had to interrupt our conference, which included the presence of Dr. Jim Nelson (author of Embodiment, and a pro-gay heterosexual seminary professor), to strategize about what would happen if they tried to remove us forcibly. They never did. But the whole experience was sometimes referred to as "Camp Letts Not."

That was one of the dramas that characterized the week, but there was another. Tensions between male and female leadership in UFMCC are always present but more visible at certain times than at others. AIDS was just barely beginning to be understood and experienced at this point.

One of the dynamics that UFMCC leaders, both clergy and lay, always have to deal with is the heterosexism that creeps into our interactions. Because we are mostly gay and lesbian in UFMCC, we somehow imagine that we are *exempt* from the dangers of falling into heterosexist roles and patterns. Well, forget it! Whenever men and women in UFMCC work together, we have to face and identify the inevitable ways in which heterosexual patterns subconsciously emerge. Women assistant pastors in UFMCC will often find themselves playing the role of wife and mommy to men pastors. Or sometimes, just for variety's sake, women and men will switch roles, but the roles are still present.

One of the continuous strains in UFMCC has been the way women often fall into the role of taking care of the men. This can be either overt or subtle. In the age of AIDS, the pressure to take care of men has been incredible for women in our church. These pressures have driven some women away. But they existed prior to AIDS as well. Women were support staff, confidantes, for men. Sometimes we covered up for them. We defended them. We endured sexism from them. We educated them. But by 1982, a lot of the first generation of UFMCC lesbian clergy were already weary and discouraged. We were part of the first wave of women clergy in significant numbers in the history of the Church! Many of us who were brilliant, creative, outstanding preachers and teachers felt like failures as leaders. We thought of this as a personal issue and not enough as a political, historical, and systemic problem. We blamed ourselves.

All the models of pastoring were male. All the books on how to pastor successfully were by men, for men. Somewhere, inside us, we felt we would never be good enough. And as proud lesbian she-women, we could never admit this to each other! We were tough! We were superwomen! Well, it was a lie. But a miracle happened at Camp Letts. We started talking about it. Like the old consciousness-raising groups of the early women's movement, we began talking about it. Not that we hadn't talked about sexism or inclusive language or all of that for a long time. But now we were talking to each other. So the women got together. And it made some of the men nervous. Some of us were thrilled that Dr. Nelson was there. However, we were also furious that when a straight white man said the very same things women had been saying for years, the men believed him! Suddenly, dealing with sexism was an *in* thing to do. So, the women withdrew. The men felt abandoned because, well, we abandoned them. Not forever, but for this time.

It started the first night when a few of us sat around in the dorm and one of the women just started crying about her anger, about a particular man she was having a conflict with, about things she felt hopeless about. We were in a circle, more or less, and I said, "Why don't we pray for you?" A novel idea—clergywomen actually praying for each other. Then I thought (emboldened now), "Why don't we kind of *lay hands on you* while we pray?" Uh-oh. This sounded a little weird. Isn't that the stuff Pentecostals did? But we did it. As we laid lesbian hands on her and began praying, something happened. A sound came from this woman's throat. An explosion of rage and pain, like a huge boil being excised. She sobbed in relief. We were stunned; we held her. It was sort of like we'd landed in the middle of someone else's group therapy session. Then, a little timidly, another lesbian clergywoman said, "Me next." She then told of the pain in her relationship with male colleagues, of her desire to pastor her own church, of her self-doubt. Her fears of her own radical feminism. So, we took turns praying for her. Once again the explosive rage and pain and relief.

I'm not entirely clear about the sequence of things after this point. We skipped dinner, after praying for two or three more women, and then took a break to go to worship services. But we couldn't wait to get back to our new-found experience.

We took over one dorm room, which meant that some women, who felt a little uneasy, decided to move. We tried to negotiate this so that no one would feel pressured to participate or excluded if they did want to participate. I took the lead in suggesting methods of doing the work. Along the way women would interrupt me, correct my mistakes, challenge me, take over from me. Laywomen and clergywomen came to the circle for healing. We eventually split into two circles, the demand was so great. At about three in the morning, my legs got so cramped and sore someone massaged them. But I felt like I had boundless energy and insight. I didn't need to drink or eat or sleep. We continued to pray, cry, laugh, hold each other, push, back off, try again, pray, heal for hours. All night long, in fact. Some attended part of the conference during the next day, some took naps. But then we got right back to it that night. Women came for healing of their careers, for their churches, but mostly for *themselves*. They began to talk; about incest and abuse in ways I had never heard in my life. This prefigured all the revelations about childhood trauma that we would continue to hear about for the next ten years.

It was incredible, to say the least. We stopped worrying about the men. We turned the full force, power, and beauty of our spiritual energy and lives toward each other. We glowed with a delicious sense of having spent ourselves on each other. We lavished our time and love and touch and listening energy on each other's bodies and spirits. *We loved each other into speech and wholeness*, to amplify Nelle Morton's powerful phrase, "hearing into speech."[5]

There were moments of unbearable pain and stuckness, and women struggled with their fears of telling the whole truth—fears that if they told the truth, no one would believe them. That there would be no one to face it with them. That they would be alone and comfortless before the terror of their past. But we weren't alone. Women who had never laid hands on each other in prayer discovered how gifted we were. We experienced, we failed, we tried again. Some dropped out at different points, needing to rest, needing to grieve quietly, needing to give themselves safe space. No one interfered with the natural rhythms of our comings and goings. We were learning together: we tried to be compassionate. Lucia Chappelle, who participated in this experience, wrote the following new hymn to a familiar Christmas carol:

> *Silent night, raging night,*
> *Women weep at their plight.*
> *Circling nurturers comfort give*
> *Offering new kinds of spiritual gifts.*
> *Christ's new Body is born,*
> *Christ's new Body is born.*
>
> *Silent night, raging night,*
> *Ne'er before, such a sight.*
> *Christian lesbians hand in hand*
> *Many theories, one mighty band.*
> *Christ's new Body is born,*
> *Christ's new Body is born.*[6]

Many women looked at those days and nights as a turning point. Sometimes, when I think about it, I long for the intensity of that time that time of a door opening. Some of the learning we did that night survives in the pastoral ministry of dozens of lesbians (and those they've mentored) who have continued to practice the healing arts over the I decade, especially in MCC. I think those healing arts stood us in good stead during the worst of the first phase of Aids. And, there were moments in hospices and hospitals and homes, when, with families and friends, praying for the dying was a similar experience of transcendence and power in the midst of suffering.

Also, in the last ten years or so, the gay male faerie movement, Joseph Kramer's work, Mark Thompson's writing and work, and, more recently, Michael Kelly and the Rainbow sash movement in Australia, have made those very important links between same-sex eroticism, spirituality and healing. As 'erotic contemplatives' (Kelly's phrase), we have a great reservoir of strength and power in our connections with each other and with the divine. And, this connection is not just a present one, but an historical one in our community.

I still think, though, that lesbians, and lesbian clergy in MCC (or the mainline churches) are reluctant to give to each other freely and completely. I think we still have a lot of rediscovering of ourselves and our personal and collective power. With feminism at a very low ebb these days, lesbians are running AIDS agencies, most of the gay and lesbian organizations. We've been co-opted and mainstreamed into the gay and lesbian movement, and life in general. I think we still long for and are afraid of the power we have with each other. If we did completely support and give to each other, would we have to face all the pain of the deprivation we have experienced? Would we have to change the way we do everything? The way we feel about everything? There is something about the power of same-sex eroticism and camaraderie that is essential to the survival of our species in our world. Will the world or the Church ever be able to receive that gift? Will we?

### Gift Number 3   The Humorous Messenger

The "camp meeting" at Camp Letts I described in the previous section included raucous, uninhibited laughter. The healing properties of the physical activity of laughing have been well documented. Also well documented is the place of humor in the gay and lesbian culture.

I can think of no other protest or civil rights movement that has been accompanied by so much self-reflective humor. Mark Thompson writes about this as if it were almost an ethnic or genetic gay and lesbian characteristic in his essay "Children of Paradise: A Brief History of Queens:"

> "The role of the fool, the trickster, the contrary one capable of turning a situation inside out, is one of the most enduring of all archetypes. Often cross-dressed, or adorned with both masculine and feminine symbols, these merry pranksters chase through history, holding up a looking glass to human folly."[7]

"Holding up a looking glass to human folly": sometimes humor is a response to the deadly power of tragedy, and its attempts to rob us of whatever joy or hope we possess. I can never forget the chant that would inevitably start at AIDS demonstrations when stone-faced police officers would arrive with their prophylactic yellow rubber gloves allegedly to keep themselves from catching AIDS while dragging us away to jail:

> Your gloves don't match your shoes,
> your gloves don't match your shoes!

Nothing about AIDS is funny. Or about the ignorance of the state and those who police it. But these chanters saw something funny in the fanciful, ignorant projections of their persecutors and made fun of them. That humorous way of turning the tables, of laughing in the face of insults, is simultaneously disarming and empowering.

Sacramento, California, is not known for its architectural or aesthetic beauty. So when hundreds of thousands of gay and lesbian protestors took over the capital in October of 1991, a clever chant mocking the stereotype of gay interior decorators was designed for the occasion:

We're here! We're queer! Let's redecorate!

One of the worst slanders directed toward gays and lesbians is that there is something inherently sad, lonely, and pitiful about our lifestyle. Or if there is any humor, it must be self-destructive, à la *Boys in the Band*. I've known thousands of gay and lesbian and bisexual people. The sad and lonely stuff is about oppression, not about sexuality. And the cure for that is coming out. Not that we don't have the same human complaints as everyone else, or our moments or moods, or neurotic friends!

While at the 1991 WCC General Assembly in Australia, we were treated to an evening of local Australian entertainment outdoors in a nearby park, and around 3,000 people were present. About ten women from the Christian Lesbian Collective came down from Sydney to support us, as did UFMCC folks from all over Australia and even a few people from New Zealand. I was particularly touched by the Christian Lesbian Collective, none of whom I had ever met before, who came to support an out lesbian speaking at the Assembly (me). Some of those women became friends over time, and continue to bravely struggle for lesbian inclusion in the Uniting Church of Australia and other mainstream churches.

In all, about 30 gays and lesbians sat together that evening on the lawn amidst the three thousand, thrilled to have found each other in this big crowd on that beautiful continent. Those of us from the U.S. delegation were especially glad to have local gay and lesbian support for our presence at the WCC assembly.

We lounged on the grass together, sharing food, stories, clowning, showing off, introducing ourselves. I sat on the edge of our crowd next to a group of Korean Protestants. The man sitting next to me kept staring at me. We introduced ourselves, just as the program was beginning. He kept asking me questions, and I was a little annoyed at the time. So, probably in hopes of shutting down the conversation, I came out to him about UFMCC. But this only made him want to talk more. He wanted to know how I knew I was a lesbian. How my family felt about it. His questions felt awkward and intrusive. I finally asked him if we could arrange to have a longer conversation when it was easier to talk. He froze up at the suggestion.

And then I saw it, that familiar look of fear on his face, the look of a closeted gay person. I saw the desperate, strained, starved look, utterly humorless. He finally looked at me squarely and said, "Are you happy?"

I was going to answer just for myself, when a familiar sound caught my attention. It was Rev. Steve Pieters (at the time the UFMCC AIDS Director, and one of our delegates to the WCC) waving his muscled arms above his head in a kind of dance, just screaming with laughter about something, the way Steve can be hunky and nelly in the same moment. Everyone around him was in on the joke. They were laughing, hugging, gesturing wildly. These people who had been strangers just half an hour ago were having the time of their lives. I simply turned to my new friend and said, "Do they look happy?"

He looked over the scene (how could you miss it?) and said with the barest hint of a smile, "Yes."

"All of them are gay," I said.

His mouth just opened, wordless. "I see," he finally said, sighing. A little tear was in the corner of his eye. He then felt the need to turn back to his group for the rest of the evening. Though we passed each other many times during the assembly, he never looked at me or acknowledged my presence again.

### Gift Number 4   Our Shamanistic Gifts of Creativity, Originality, Art, Magic and Theater

One of the features in my "pastor's bag of tricks" is my magic act. It's not a real magic act. It's pure spoof, zany and a little bit mad. I started doing it at clergy conferences late at night when I was bored or when I felt my colleagues needed entertaining (sort of like my own version of USO). Then it just took on a life of its own! I occasionally perform it while visiting UFMCC churches or at congregational meetings.

I had loved dressing up and entertaining as a child. But not in the usual ways. Halloween was one of my favorite times. I'd usually dress in some kind of male drag, and then I'd dress up both my brothers and anything else that would stay still long enough. I wrote plays for our neighbor kids and loved to fantasize about being a performer. I didn't feel pretty or feminine, but I knew I could make people laugh. Mostly I liked making myself laugh.

Once in a while, at serious moments in church, I have a nearly uncontrollable impulse to break into the magic act. Preaching and leading worship and consecrating the elements are all magical, and some times they just cry out for a *lighter touch*.

There is this persistent stereotype of "gays and the theater." Gay musical-comedy queens. Lesbian softball as performance art. One of the functions of gay and lesbian people is that we are the *in-between* ones. Judy Grahn says (in *Another Mother Tongue*) that in times of great social transformation and upheaval, we carry messages across gender lines. We are the *berdache* (Native American word for gay male or crossdresser) who patch up broken relationships. We are the go-betweens when there are disputes. We are the mediators of conflict and culture. In some ways, we are those who intercede, who create the pathway for change, for moving into the next era.

I had a wonderful opportunity to organize gay people to exercise this gift at the WCC General Assembly. One of the contexts of the assembly in Canberra in 1991 was the Gulf War. The WCC decided to hold a vigil to pray for the end of the war.

The U.S. delegation (the largest, with 600 people) was to lead the closing hour of the vigil at six in the morning. (This was the Sunday morning before the emotional communion with the Lima Liturgy.) In organizing for the vigil and our participation, Joan Campbell, General Secretary of the NCC, had asked for a few volunteers. Well, I knew that meetings like this, no one really wants to volunteer for such things. All my ecu-terrorist training kicked in, and I volunteered. Joan didn't flinch at all and I was appointed to the committee, which included some U.S. denominational leaders and WCC delegates.

Our planning committee met briefly outside the worship tent. Rev. Kit Cherry had made some helpful suggestions. No one else seemed to have any ideas. The rest of the committee's idea of the good use of an hour of vigil time was to read more and more boring statements about how we hate the war. So, to work we went! UFMCC folks (and some closeted gay members in the group) suggested that we open with a Native American drum call to worship. Then, after some brief testimony and prayer, we could invite people forward for anointing with oil.

We decided to use oil because it was a biblical symbol for healing and for *brotherhood and sisterhood.* We chose Psalms 133:1-2:

> How very good and pleasant it is when brothers and sisters live together in unity!
> It is like the precious oil on the head, running down upon the beard, on the beard of Aaron.

This would also allow us to use, with a sense of irony, a symbol of the painful reality that the buying and selling of *oil* was at the heart of horrible war.

People seemed to like our suggestion, mostly because they were stressed and tired to come up with anything else. Those participating then told me they didn't exactly know how to anoint with oil, so we did a practice session. Actually, I didn't remember anyone ever teaching me how do it. It was like I was born knowing how to do this. We suggested using the conference theme as an anointing blessing, "Come, Holy Spirit renew your whole creation," although I explained that the pastors might want to be free just to pray or bless freestyle, if they felt so moved. Most of them looked utterly terrified by that suggestion.

Then we began to search for blessed oil. No one seemed to have any. I had certainly not brought any with me from the United States. No one on the worship team staff at Canberra had any or knew where to find some. Finally, one of the staff "gophers" told me he knew where to get oil! Kit Cherry and I decided to use her empty film cases as makeshift oil vials, and we got UFMCC people to hold the vials for the blessors during the time of anointing (so that they wouldn't get distracted by the fact that the oil was in film cases!).

I waited forever for this guy to come back with the oil. Finally, he found me: he had the happy look of one who has successfully completed his mission. He handed me a bottle of baby oil. Baby oil! I could just imagine how distracting it would be to be anointing or anointed with the smell of baby oil all around. Can you imagine having this solemn service in the WCC worship tent—and then anointing people who suddenly feel like taking a nap? "They didn't have any olive oil?" I whined. "Olive oil?" he said blankly. Holy oil is not supposed to smell like babies' bottoms! But ever resourceful, our gay spirit rose to the occasion. Steve Pieters just happened to have some frankincense with him. Sure—don't you know people who carry frankincense around with them all the time?! I think the fact that Steve just happened to be carrying frankincense reinforced my suspicion that those Wise Men had to have been gay.

So I mixed the baby oil and frankincense and put the mixture in the film cases. This did change the smell, well, at least a little. Then we blessed the oil in preparation for the service.

I was comforted by the belief that not very many people would show up at six in the morning for this event. WRO-ONG! Probably over 500 people were there when it started.

The drumming began, the prayers were said, and then I read the Psalm and talked about how we might transform and restore the image of oil for ourselves that day. We needed to anoint each other and the whole world that morning. And we did. Joan Campbell, Bishop Edmund Browning, myself, and six or seven others began anointing the crowd while an African-American seminarian woman sang, 'There is balm in Gilead, to make the wounded whole." Edmund Browning really needed that anointing, after having refused to give the President of the United States (George Bush, Episcopalian) his blessing to bomb Baghdad. There was eventually some White House retaliation against Browning for his refusal to go along with the war. Browning probably knew, even then, that it might cost him. And he, Browning, had worked hard to rally the religious community to seek other solutions to the crisis with Iraq and Kuwait. To no avail. For church leaders, some of whom had rallied against the US participation in the Vietnam War, this was a horribly depressing state of affairs. They, we, felt hopeless and helpless.

So, when the exiled Bishop of Baghdad came forward that morning (having barely escaped with his life) to be anointed by Bishop Browning, the room just broke open in solidarity with our pain and our helplessness. Some were too overcome to keep anointing. They collapsed in sobs, on the floor, in their chairs. People wept, prayed, hugged, as the mournful sounds of that spiritual continued. Gay and lesbian delegates to the WCC came forward for anointing, hugged me, and came out to me on the spot. The tent was filled with the power and presence of the God who wanted us to transform not only the WCC but the world, who makes a way where there is no way, who longs to turn swords into plowshares.

Many people spoke to me about how moving and *right on* that liturgy was. I felt a bit mystified. To me, it felt so familiar, so ordinary. Not the context, of course. That was overwhelming and extraordinary. But the liturgy, the anointing. The *sensing of the moment*, inventing liturgy to move and express the fullness of the moment, was what we experience frequently at Metropolitan Community Churches. It made me realize how much I take UFMCC and the gifts of gay and lesbian people for granted. And how grateful we were to have to opportunity to be a servant of the Church in that moment. And I loved the subtext of the baby oil and frankincense and film case mischief. The humor and joy and the making do with what we have. As Harry Hay says, "turning hand-me-downs into visions of loveliness."[8]

There is also that strange phenomenon we affectionately call our *gaydar*: the *radar* that, across a crowded room, often allows gay and lesbian people to identify each other. It is not foolproof, mind you.

At one very tense NCC meeting (in Cleveland, Ohio, 1992), UFMCC and members of the gay and lesbian caucuses pooled our resources and set up a hospitality suite to welcome NCC delegates, create some safe space for ourselves, and have all our literature available. Not many NCC folks showed up. But I began to notice that people were disappearing from our visitors' table and excusing themselves to "person" the suite. Soon the word came back that although the NCC was not availing itself of our hospitality, the gay and lesbian hotel employees were! There was a party going on up there, and as the employees ate up all our food, MCC people shared with them the good news that God does love gay and lesbian people. From that moment on, during the course of the NCC meeting, I could often look across the ballroom and see hotel employees serving coffee to bishops and delegates while rolling their eyes at us!

Harry Hay also reports that "the biologist, Julian Huxley, over half century ago pointed out that no negative trait [and we know, in biology negative trait is one that does not reproduce itself] ever appears in a given species millennia after millennia unless it in some way serves the survival of that species. We are a species variant with a particular characteristic adaptation in consciousness whose time has come!"[9] Could we be a wonderful human adaptation that excels in the gifts of humor, truth-telling and magic of all kinds?

**Gift Number 5   Made in the Image of God**

On a church visit to All God's Children MCC in Minneapolis, I witnessed a new phenomenon: a gay men's softball team. Now, lesbian softball is legendary and an undisputed part of lesbian culture in the United States. But a gay male team? MCC Minneapolis has three teams: two are lesbian, and one is composed of young gay men with shaved, punk haircuts, earrings, and muscled bodies (who want to be lesbians when they grow up?). They have a very cute team name: The Altared Boys, and great T-shirts that say:

MADE IN THE IMAGE OF GOD—
not necessarily
YOUR IMAGE OF GOD!

I believe that gay and lesbian people contribute to a more complete picture of God. If human beings are made in the image of God, then that includes gay men and lesbians. What about us rounds out the image, do you suppose? The God who invented truth, who is always *coming out* (another synonym for revelation?).

I've always felt that God has a sense of humor. Much of the humor in the Bible has long since been lost in the translation, quite literally. But "he [sic] who sits in the heavens laughs" (Psalms 2:4). Sometimes I think God plays with me, and we have had some private jokes. For a long time I was afraid to say that out loud. It seemed so grandiose and self-absorbed. I was too sophisticated really to think of God in those affectionate, personal terms.

Sometimes it's just the incredible, illogical synchronicity of things. During one of the worst years of my life (1977), I was driving in the wee hours of the morning from Fort Wayne, Indiana, to Detroit, Michigan, coming home from a preaching engagement. I had recently ended a four-year relationship that had been deteriorating for some time. In addition, there were some nightmarish events and problems that had affected the church. I was exhausted, demoralized, and felt, in the words of Al-Anon literature, "unwanted, unloved, and alone" —and sorry for myself. I turned on the radio and heard a new song: it was Billy Joel's "Just the Way You Are." Later I would learn that Billy was from my home town of Hicksville, New York. Billy's Long Island accent was poignantly familiar and tugged at me on that lonely road—and the words, the saxophone. I changed the station, and the song came on again. That startled me. A new popular tune, I guess! I listened to the words again, full of sweet assurances. I began to have this eerie feeling of not being alone in the car. I could feel the tightness in my chest relax and the sadness and depression lift for a moment. In a little while I turned the dial again—and there it was again. This time it scared me. OK, it's you. You love me. The tears came, I started laughing, "OK, OK, OK. OK, God, you love me. You want to talk to me."

But it didn't stop there. It seemed that every time I walked into a room where a radio was playing, it was on. Other people even noticed it. This went on for months and months. Paula and I were walking through Boston Commons the following summer (we had met just three weeks after my drive from Fort Wayne that night, redeeming the year for me), and a guy was playing that song on a xylophone! Even today, that sweet song appears and interrupts me, especially if I'm feeling a little unwanted, a little unloved, or alone. I don't pretend to understand it; I don't, but I'm trying to accept it. The words and tune just sort of befriended me, as a precious gift from a God who thinks I'm too sophisticated for my own good a lot of the time.

Now, it's one thing to claim that God might actually tolerate or accept gay and lesbian people; it's quite another to claim that people might be able to see God in and through *us* sometimes.

Our church, MCC L.A., had a sort of nervous breakdown about this in the fall of 1989. It was a difficult time. I had been on a 30 day fast (to pull the church together and call attention to the fact that we might be in danger of losing our church property partly because banks won't give mortgages to churches, much less gay and lesbian churches), followed by gall bladder surgery. I had been out for seven weeks. The church had been worried about me. We were successful in saving the property, able to move into our building and to raise enough funds to keep us going for a while, until we finally got that new loan years later.

But MCC L.A. folks were *weary*. A young, brilliant student clergy was writing the liturgy and preaching for my first Sunday back, All Saints Day. He and a small committee had designed a very innovative gay and lesbian All Saints' liturgy that they knew might be a little controversial. Jim (the student clergy) thought I had seen it before it "went to press." I had not. Ten minutes before the services began, deacons came roaring into my office telling me I had to *pull* the liturgy. I finally got to see it. In the call to worship it said, "O lesbian God, O gay and gracious God... " It was not my style to pull the rug out from under student clergy, even if I think they're being wrong headed about something. I knew that some of the more conservative and evangelical gay and lesbian MCC Los Angeles folks would be disturbed by these words, but I didn't think it was a matter of life and death. So I got up at the beginning of the service, tried just to acknowledge the conflict and to help us relax and get through it.

Well, it just got worse. I had no idea how frightening and devastating it would be for some people to hear this liturgy. Some folks were oblivious, some loved the liturgy, but many were simply horrified at the phrase "lesbian God."

Part of the problem was that those from evangelical and conservative backgrounds often have difficulty with metaphorical language about God that you cannot document in the Bible. And another part of it was leftover guilt, shame, and doubt about how God feels about us.

I tried to say, "Yes, but you call God the *rock* of your salvation, and you *know* God is not really a rock...." But for them there was a difference between familiar metaphors and this new one. They were partly terrified that someone (some visitor to our church, perhaps) would believe that they were not worshiping the God of the Bible, the God of Jesus, but that somehow this phrase meant they were worshiping their own sexuality. This had been an early stereotype of UFMCC. That we were not really a church, that we were a cover for a gay "social club" or sex club, or that we were just using the veneer of "church" to justify ourselves. All these were (and still are) painful misrepresentations of our church, which we continually battled. Also we struggled not to be so exclusively gay or lesbian—so we were afraid that heterosexual people would not feel welcomed and included by this liturgy. For some people, the articulation of "gay God" seemed like self-worship, like blasphemy, like a betrayal. Too exclusive, too *out there*.

Interestingly enough, however, it was "lesbian God" and not "gay God" that was attacked. At least with the metaphor "gay God," God was still male. That told me a lot.

I tried to communicate, counsel, and teach about metaphorical language about God. For some of the people who had been upset, this helped. For others it didn't. Some wanted me to punish Jim, the student clergy, which I would not do. Some used this event to dump all their fears and angers about the fast on me. Some wanted me to say that the lesbian God thing was a terrible mistake. I did believe that not preparing the congregation for that liturgy was a tactical mistake, and I would have done it differently if I'd had the opportunity. But I could not say what some of them wanted to hear: that comparing God to a lesbian or a gay man was a *terrible* mistake.

When I tried to help them hear that God is everything *good* that gay and lesbian people are, just as God is everything good that a rock is, or a lily of the valley, or a shepherd, it just didn't get through.

I tried to say that we are not less like God than a rock, or a tree, or a heterosexual person. But when I tried to communicate this, I often hit a brick wall—a brick wall called internalized homophobia. My efforts to name it were met with scoffing, denial, and incredibly painful statements such as "calling God a lesbian is the worst thing you could ever call him [sic]." This was spoken by a lesbian.

It broke my heart, and it drove Jim away from the church for perhaps the last time (he'd been a Lutheran seminarian before he came to UFMCC). It took a long time for us to understand and process that trauma and to understand how deep the wounds of internalized self-hatred are in our community. When we are very affirming about being gay or lesbian, or about being made in the image of God, we simply scare ourselves to death. Somehow, when we see our sexuality as part of our connection to the image of God, we feel we will be accused of making God in our image. (Or we accuse ourselves before anyone else has a chance to!)

## Our Spiritual Gifts

These, then, are some of our gifts: truth telling, most especially in the form of coming out; same-sex erotic friendship as a cultural antidote to the eroticization of dominance and dependence; being willing to be the humorous messenger; creativity and magic; and contributing to a fuller image of God. All of these, in their own way, are spiritual gifts. But are there other more explicitly spiritual gifts that gay men and lesbians might give to the Church? What might be some positive elements in gay and lesbian spirituality?

### Pro-life Spirituality

I would like to use Mary Daly's method of the "righteous rip-off" for this concept! It seems to me that those who have taken the label "pro-life" are often pro-life only up until birth. (They don't support a nuclear freeze, an end to capital punishment, gun control, or universal day care, for example.) Also, gay and lesbian people have been viewed negatively because we don't reproduce—as if that makes us somehow antifamily, antilife. The fact that we don't reproduce without a great deal of extra effort and inconvenience most of the time means that when we do have children, we want them. And we are willing to care for them. Also, many gay and lesbian people raise other people's offspring, as we always have. (How many straight people were raised by "unmarried" aunts or uncles, many of whom were gay or lesbian?)

In addition, gay and lesbian people are wonderful aunts, uncles, and godparents to millions of children. We assist parents, providing backup parenting, adult supervision, and companionship for their children. Also, gay and lesbian people are not just human-centered—we dote on our pets and are historically an earth-friendly tribe. We are overrepresented in the helping and caring professions and in environmental and other life-centered movements. The fact that we do not ordinarily reproduce as a result of our sexual activity means that we are helping in the efforts to control population! Overpopulation is never pro-life: it is pro-poverty. We are indeed a people who are singing for our lives: Yes—who know that silence equals death and that action equals life. Reclaiming our love for life and our life-giving self-image is a great spiritual gift we can give to the world and to the Church.

### An Irreverent Piety

We are probably in a good position to hold up the mirror of reflection to the Church especially. We are, after all, the "in-between" folks. We've been both very much on the inside of the Church (as its organists, choir directors, pastors, board members, deacons, bishops) and on the outside, trying to learn how to "embrace the exile," in John Fortunato's famous phrase.

At that same WCC meeting in Australia in 1992, Steve Pieters tells of a conversation with an Australian Anglican. Steve was wearing a lavender clergy shirt and waiting in the lobby for a meeting to begin. An older Australian delegate approached him and said, "In our church, when someone wears that color clergy shirt it means they are a bishop!" To which Steve replied, "In our church, it means we are gay!" (That's not entirely accurate, but Steve was being playful.) The woman did *not* skip a beat and rejoined, "I guess that's what it means in our church, too!"

Over the years people have sometimes commented on my irreverence. Frankly, I hold back a lot. Not because I think God will be offended but because I don't want to be more misunderstood than I already am. But I see irreverence mostly as play. When you really trust someone, you can kid them. You know how far to go. I feel like I have that kind of relationship with God.

My grandfather, part Indian and part reluctant Baptist, had that kind of relationship with God. In one of the few private conversations we ever had, he told me on the way home from church one day that I "should not take this church stuff too seriously." He went on to say that it seemed to him that anyone (namely, Jesus) who would change water into wine must have enjoyed himself now and then. Don't let them take all the joy out of life. "Them," I figured, meant preachers and other religious folks. My grandfather already knew that I was attracted to this "church stuff," and he worried about me because of it! I think he is still a source of my irreverence and my desire for a lighter touch at times.

Church ought to be a place where people are loved, comforted and uplifted, but also a place where we are shocked, shaken and turned around. Also, a place where we can laugh. I'm not talking about giggling or chuckling but deep, roll-in-the-aisles laughing. Not every Sunday perhaps, but frequently. In the Middle Ages, it was the custom to begin every Easter Sunday morning sermon with a joke. It was the day above all days when we were to laugh in church, to laugh at the devil who had been utterly defeated and outsmarted. I tell a joke every Easter Sunday at MCC L.A. In reminds me of the primacy of joy and laughter in the spiritual pantheon.

In most UFMCC churches, there will be laughter—in some, a great deal of laughter. Maybe this started because many of us were nervous about being in church and being ourselves all at the same time. Some UFMCC services, even in the sophisticated ones, can have just a hint of the barroom rowdiness that is a leftover from the time when noisy, crowded bars were the only places we were more or less permitted to meet. For some people, UFMCC is the only place where they are out of the closet or where they can hold their lover's hand in public. And we have endless arguments about that all the time. What is proper church etiquette in a gay and lesbian church that is open to everyone? Why do people sometimes behave like they are in a bar when they are in a church? Well, it's a cultural remnant, I'm sure. I think. And it helped make UFMCC, at least in its first decade or so, a little less threatening to people who were frightened of or allergic to too much church. It also probably put off a lot of more middle class people for whom MCC was too "out," and rough and tumble (which in many places in the world it still is.)

Part of the theological menu available at UFMCC includes a healthy dose of charismatic theology, worship and piety, hopefully with out the accompanying narrowness and fundamentalism. This is because UFMCC's roots are thoroughly working class, and many of our members are from that background.

Every year MCC Long Beach, California, hosts a charismatic conference. I try never to miss it. There is nothing quite like seeing several hundred gay, lesbian, and bisexual charismatics (or those dabbling in it for the weekend) worshiping, weeping, singing, holding, sweating, and hugging each other, unashamed of their love for God and each other. There is often dancing in the spirit, speaking in tongues, prophecy, and other gifts of the spirit in evidence.

One year, the year after the "lesbian God" controversy at MCC Los Angeles—also the year I had just lost 30 pounds (and a gall bladder) in a fast—I attended the Saturday evening service at the charismatic conference. I was having a difficult time. I was recovering from surgery and a church fight. There were many in the church, my family, and the Fellowship who did not understand why I had fasted. I had had a lot of support, but I had also been through a lot of hell that year. Some questioned my judgment and my sanity.

The guest speaker at the Charismatic Conference was a powerful, heterosexual woman, Erla Duncan, known in charismatic circles for her gifts of knowledge, prophecy, and healing. She is a short woman with a big voice and a rather imposing presence. Erla had taken a lot of heat in her ministry for not condemning gay and lesbian people, and for being willing to teach and preach in our churches. I met her for just a few minutes before the service. It was amazing to watch her. She'd call on you (in front of 300 people!) and just start talking about you to you or prophesying about you. Neither you nor she had any idea of what was going to happen. She'd talk, and people would begin to cry, or shout, or pray.

That night she pointed to me. I stood, feeling like a very nervous six-year-old. She prophesied that I would be given opportunities to speak in arenas of national importance, and lots of other things. But then she paused and said, in a booming voice, "But, oh, the devil hates you! In fact, they have weekly meetings about you!" When she said that to me, my face reddened, but the crowd roared. And then I began to laugh. And I couldn't stop laughing. In fact, I laughed all the way home that night. I laughed on the way to church the next day. I laughed about it for weeks, off and on. What a great, sweeping, overwhelming relief!

I did not grow up with theological language that ever talked much about the *devil*, and when I first encountered it in people at UFMCC, it made me nervous. I still haven't sorted out all those issues. But I do know that God has enemies, whatever you choose to call them or it. And if I am God's friend, those forces and folks will also see me as their enemy. I do believe that if you "resist the devil, he [sic] will flee from you" (Jas. 4:7); but first, he or she will try to make life miserable for you. Once I was willing to face that some of the hell I had been going through was because I had resisted evil, because I had tried to move some terribly stubborn mountains, I was so relieved. Like all folks (including ancient shamans) who do such things, I had to pay a price for it. But ultimately, I was and am safe.

Erla Duncan's word to me that night was God's word to me, delivered in the kind of humorous, irreverent way I could recognize. The devil mad at me? What a great tribute! Weekly meetings! Hah! Her strange (for me) words empowered and emboldened me, and healed me in the laughter they provoked.

## A Spirituality That Makes Creative Use of Suffering

I remember reading Edmund Bergler's book *Homosexuality: Disease or Way of Life?* when I was in college.[10] Bergler's answer to his own question was definitely "disease"! One of the *seven* (deadly?) character defects that he felt were common to all homosexuals was "injustice collecting." This meant that we stayed up at night obsessing and whining about all the terrible things people had done to us. Of the seven, this is the only one I remember. Perhaps because it stung the most, as if there might be a grain of truth in it for me. Something else to dislike myself for. It touched on all my repressed pain, hurt and memories of suffering. Did I cherish those memories just a little too much? Was that cherishing a response to never having been able to express them, to air them? They were a part of my secret life.

**91**

I also did have enough sophistication even then to see that Bergler was playing the blame-the-victim game once again. Homosexuals don't have real suffering, he was saying—it's all either imagined or exaggerated, or they've brought it on themselves and, therefore, it is suffering they deserve.

We deserve to suffer for our "crimes against nature." And because nature herself didn't seem to punish us enough (although, of course, some have wanted to see AIDS this way), the Church and state has to do it for her. But was it not a crime against nature to burn millions of women accused of witchcraft in the Middle Ages, or millions of gay men and lesbians in the Holocaust?[11]

I feel very reluctant to assign meaning to human (or other) suffering—like those who say that everything that happens is "God's will." I fully and completely understand the human desire to do that, to explain, justify, *package* suffering—especially to give suffering a purpose. But I think that most suffering is terribly arbitrary and that part of its painfulness is that much of it is unnecessary, preventable, and pointless.

Nevertheless, suffering may have its uses. In a way, I view suffering as spiritual compost. It becomes the soil in which many things may grow: bitterness, rage, despair, loneliness, hopelessness; or conversely, compassion, tenderness, openness, kindness, forbearance, patience.

What grows in our compost heaps of accumulated suffering? It is, after all, what grows, not the compost itself, that may have meaning, purpose, even redemptive value. And in saying that, I do not mean to imply anything in the way of an equation. The juice may not always be worth the squeeze. Or more crudely and irreverently, the screwing you're getting may not be worth the screwing you're getting. Not all suffering is good compost. But now and then we get a glimpse of a divine economy that may be large enough to incorporate and heal the suffering of the world. Every now and then.

I met Lew Adams shortly after I became pastor of MCC L.A. He was an "old-timer" in two senses. He was almost 70 years old, and he had been a member of MCC L.A. for at least 15 years.

Lew came to my office, troubled because he hadn't been baptized and felt he should be. But, he told me, he didn't feel worthy, and he had a hang-up about it. It was a requirement that you be baptized in order to be a member of UFMCC, but somehow that had been overlooked when Lew had become a member.

Lew's best friends frequently "pestered" Lew about this baptism thing, and, well, he thought he probably should do it. But Lew told me he couldn't because it reminded him of his father. Lew's father had been a crazy, abusive, religious fanatic, who starved his children, subjected them to countless beatings, and who had a very bizarre sectarian fundamentalist "Christian" theology. Lew had hated his father. He'd had to eat out of garbage cans as a child. He ran away at age 14 and went to the Philippines. When he was old enough, he joined the navy. He ended up becoming a victim of the March of Bataan in the Philippines. During his captivity, he personally buried hundreds of soldiers who had died of starvation. Lew was convinced that the only reason he survived was because of his early *childhood training through suffering*. He could eat garbage, he could do whatever it took to survive. Lew volunteered for many things at the church and had a small circle of friends. He was compassionate, serious, and could not bear for anyone to be hungry.

A few years after our conversation, he was diagnosed with AIDS. One day, when he was close to death, he told me that the last few years of his life, with AIDS, had been some of the happiest. He told me he felt fortunate to be one of the few older people with AIDS he had encountered. That unlike so many, he had lived a long life. But what amazed and shocked Lew were all the friends who had rallied to his side during his illness—mostly gay and lesbian friends from MCC L.A. who loved him, prayed with him, kept him company, took care of him. He loved coming to church and felt such a peace and joy there. Finally, just a week or so before his death, he told me he was ready to be baptized. Several friends gathered around, and there was not a dry eye. Lew had a kind of transcendent joy and presence in those last days. There was also the occasional flash of old anger or grief. It took him a whole lifetime to heal from that religious abuse, but he made it. And AIDS became a means of grace for him, as he learned to receive just a portion of the love he had offered to so many all his life. I will never forget his humility and gratitude in the face of horrific suffering. What brilliant flowers grew from this compost of suffering. In his will, Lew left the church a little insurance money that he asked us to use to help those who were in need, especially those who were hungry.

Finally, I also believe that gays and lesbians have another gift to give to the Church: a new *lens on the Bible*.

# Chapter Three—A New Lens on the Bible

It seems to me that I have always loved the Bible. But I was not always sure that it would love me back.

I remember reading the first Bible I got in Methodist Sunday school. I was determined to read it cover to cover. The print was small. I had no commentary, and weekly Sunday school lessons barely skimmed the surface of biblical stories. I read and read through long, boring, disappointing passages. Then I would come across things that were odd, frightening, or unintelligible. There were lots of endless descriptive details and hard-to-pronounce names and lists. But every now and then I stumbled on a book, chapter or verse of pure gold, worth all my perseverance. As a lonely 12-year-old, I had lots of time for this endeavor.

I loved Cranston Clayton's sermons at Hicksville Methodist Church. In his folksy Tennessee drawl, he preached a fervent, antifundamentalist, biblical social Gospel. He preached the Bible story, week after week, from a lectionary of his own creating. Anticipating the biblical illiteracy of a new generation, he retold the Bible for us. He even gave us a living Bible map: the parking lot was the Mediterranean Sea, the sanctuary was Israel, the gymnasium was Greece and Europe, and the offices were Egypt! His Bible characters were alive with poignancy and passion. I particularly appreciated that he didn't shy away from the juicier parts.

Clayton didn't care for children very much. He expected that if you were a child sitting through his sermons (which I sometimes did twice on Sundays), you'd better listen like an adult. Oh, but the way he told the stories of David and Bathsheba, Peter and Paul and Silas, Jesus and Mary Magdalene, made me want to preach.

I wanted to make people feel the way he made me feel—like I was right there in those stories, in the thick of the battles, the miracles, smelling the smoke from the burning bush, touching Jesus, feeling Deborah's strength and conviction. I loved the tears, laughter, tales of mercy and cruelty, the scandal, the surprises. He acted, agonized, mused, imagined; he painted verbal murals. Also, he seemed to have access to some mysterious repository of inside information, important details missing from the text itself. I never mistrusted his special source and the way he filled in the gaps.

So at age 14, I asked my dad to take me to talk to Clayton about becoming a preacher. Clayton just looked at me—the way people squint at people who are somehow barely visible to them. Since I knew he didn't like or notice kids and since I was female, I already knew in my heart that talking to him was a long shot. He spoke to my father mostly. "Aw," he said, "she'll be just like my daughter: go to seminary, marry some preacher, and it will all be wasted on her." My dad, who had a hard enough time just getting to the pastor's office in the first place (it made him nervous), just sat silently. When I pressed Clayton (making him talk to me), he finally grunted and gave me the name and address of a woman Methodist minister he knew about in Kansas. End of discussion.

I wrote to her the next day. She eventually wrote back. It turned out that she had been married to a minister. When he died she finally got to go to seminary and got ordained. (She was now in her 60's.) Somehow, I didn't think I could wait that long—or that I should have to. It did occur to me, in a fleeting way, that I could just marry a very old, sick man and kind of get that part out of the way real early. But that seemed grotesque to me. I had also wanted to ask Clayton why he thought God would put ideas about preaching into girls' heads if it was all just going to be a waste. And I had this other feeling that I couldn't explain and already knew not to verbalize: that being married to a man was going to be the least of my problems.

Poor Clayton. He knew the Bible real well. He just didn't know anything about young lesbians who loved the Bible. Mind you, Clayton was not above making homophobic comments. He didn't watch a lot of TV. (How could he? He had to be reading the Bible all the time and figuring out which parts we ought to hear about!) But I remember that in one sermon he talked about two brand-new TV hits. They were "doctor" shows in the early '60s: about Dr. Ben Casey and Dr. Kildare. Ben Casey was a swarthy, hypermasculine sex symbol. Dr. Kildare was blond and delicate.

Clayton decided to talk about how he didn't care for Dr. Kildare, who was too namby-pamby (read "queer"). He thought Jesus was probably more rugged (read macho), like hairy old Ben Casey. I remember my strong reaction to Clayton that morning. I took it very personally and wasn't sure why. Partly because I liked Richard Chamberlain (he played Kildare and is an openly gay man today. Clayton" suspicions were correct). I already knew that I liked boys or men better when they were pretty or a little more like girls. Hairy men kinda scared me. My dad was muscular and strong but had very little body hair (in fact, we always joked about his seven measly chest hairs). He always said it was because his father was part Indian. My dad was soft-spoken and managed, even with his mechanics scarred hands, to be gentle in his touch and manner. When I got to preach, I thought, I would make Jesus be more like Dr. Kildare. Maybe not so blond but kind of soft and pretty like Richard Chamberlain. Like my dad, or maybe like one of the women teachers I had a crush on.

Aside from the Ben Casey versus Jim Kildare fiasco, Clayton seemed right about a lot of things to me. For instance, he said that Dr. Martin Luther King, Jr. was a lot like Jesus (and, by the way, not at all like Ben Casey or Jim Kildare!) and that we ought to be a lot nicer to Catholics (in those early Vatican II years).

Robert Goss, in *Jesus Acted Up*,[1] first used the title of Phyllis Trible's book, *Texts of Terror*,[2] to identify the six Bible passages quoted by fundamentalists and uninformed Christians to condemn homosexuality.[3] These have become our "texts of terror." Their existence, combined with millennia of misinterpretation, has formed a powerful wedge, keeping lesbians and gay men from any hope of being able to celebrate and experience the story and poetry of the Bible.

In 1994, theologian Daniel Helminiak in *What the Bible* Really *Says About Homosexuality*[4] finally gave us an authoritative and accessible book to refute the faulty translations and shallow interpretations of the Bible that had been used to haunt us.

In about 1978, Dr. Norman Pittenger came to preach at MCC Detroit. He made the astonishing comment that "actually, the Bible is a greatly overrated book." This still makes me wince and laugh. All those people, over all those millennia, spending their lives poring over, studying, translating a greatly overrated book. Working hard to improve its ratlngs! Is that what we do? What I'm doing?

So is the Bible an angel I'm wrestling until it blesses me and all gay and lesbian people? Am I just locked in a lifelong "lovers' quarrel" with this book? Is it really a good book with good news for all people, including queers?

It never mattered to me whether or not the Bible was accurate as to facts. For some reason, I never equated fact and truth. It never worried me whether the Bible was literally true. Miraculously, I trusted my own heart. My heart leapt equally at the wonders of the cell, the solar system, and poetry and power of a biblical story. I love the idea of reading what ancient humans of faith felt when they saw the same creation.

Sometime during this time I saw the movie *Inherit the Wind.* I thought that God must have loved the brilliant, freethinking, doubting, questioning lovers of justice and seekers of truth like Clarence Darrow. God enjoyed them more than the mean-spirited, self-righteous ones who hated under cover of biblical infallibility. To this day, I can hardly stand to hear people arguing about teaching "creationism" at school, as if it is as viable a theory of the origin of life as Darwin's work. And poor Darwin, scientist, religious person, vilified in his own time for daring to think about the theory of evolution. Becoming the fundamentalist's punching bag.

Just for fun, I have sported that little Christian fish symbol with Darwin scrawled inside it, alongside of my Clergy sticker on my car (free parking in the emergency lot at hospitals, and occasionally help with police when being ticketed). Several times I have been accosted by mean-spirited people saying horrible things about poor, long since deceased Charles Darwin and my eternal destination. Do these people think that their rantings make Christianity look like an attractive religion?

I remember fantasizing about a special place of reconciliation in heaven for God and all the atheists and agnostics who out of love for God's creation and people, rejected perverse human notions of God especially those supposedly supported by the Bible. There was also a part of me that sometimes fantasized about a special place in hell for religious folks who used the Bible abusively to hurt, alienate, and create an atmosphere of violence toward others. That was difficult because I didn't think there really could be a hell. (Although, what did God do with Adolph Hitler?) Reluctantly, I made myself imagine their redemption, their healing. It is hard to accept this memory of my own capacity for cruel imaginings. And hard to reconcile my universalism with the endless human capacity for destruction and cruelty. Mostly I wanted to access for myself and others the mysterious, poignant, tender, sweet, funny and helpful stuff in the Bible, to loosen and lighten it up.

I had the opportunity to speak about gays and lesbians and the Bible at the college I had graduated from—Allegheny College in Meadville, Pennsylvania. I did so as an open lesbian alumna! At my lecture on "Outing the Bible," biblical literalists pounded me with a barrage of questions. They were outwardly polite, white, mostly middle-class students, wide-eyed with sincerity. I tried to understand their intensity and fear. For some of them, intellectual exchange and "agreeing to disagree" were tolerable. But others simply hammered at me rhetorically, as if trying to break me under the weight of their questions. As if just listening to them read from their Bible, I would fall down on my knees in front of them and repent! Students who I assumed (perhaps falsely) could tolerate ambiguity, fine distinction, and unresolved questions in other areas of inquiry could not do so with the Bible.

The atmosphere became ritualistic, cultlike, as one young woman repeated over and over again that if one could speculate (I had enraged her by using the word) about homosexuals in the Bible, then, one could speculate about anything in the Bible! (Which apparently would ruin it!) When I replied that I didn't find the word "speculate" to be a bad word and asked just what was she so afraid of, her intensity increased. It was as if these young students believed the Bible to be a fragile, magic, snow castle ready to melt—or a row of dominoes ready to fall with the first invading question.

For me, the Bible is an elastic, resilient friend who bounces back and even talks back when I question it. I can still see how the "biblically impaired" male student shook with rage at my really rather harmless attempts to see gays and lesbians in the Bible. The demons of homophobia screeched at me through him that night.

It would be so much easier for these students if we gays and lesbians would just continue to hate ourselves and the Bible. If like Job's wife, these students, and all who believe the way they do, could just get us to curse God and die—no problem!

But it's not their Bible or their God to control. The Bible belongs to anyone who will love it, play with it, push it to its limits, touch it, and be touched by it—and the same is true for God. The Bible must be a holy text for gays and lesbians, because we are truly human, created by the

God who created heaven and earth. We are at a critical moment on this question. Either we will believe what others have told us about the Bible, feel awful about it and ourselves (and possibly reject the Bible or devalue our selves); or, we will dare to learn and study and struggle with our own canon. The choice is ours.

From 1985 to 1987, I participated in a series of well-organized "consultations" jointly sponsored by the National Council of Churches of Christ in the U.S.A. and the UFMCC. These consultations were commissioned by the Governing Board of the NCC in the aftermath of their decision to "postpone indefinitely" their vote on UFMCC's eligibility for membership in the NCC in 1983. These three consultations were to be about subjects believed to be major areas of disagreement between UFMCC and member communions of the NCC (and, more to the point, among and between those communions). The subjects were biblical interpretations of homosexuality, the science of human sexuality, and ecclesiology (the study of the Church).

We tackled the biblical consultation first. I served as one of two UFMCC persons on the steering committee for the consultations. Our preparation included gathering the names of requested scripture scholars "in the guild" who had published on this subject and who would be willing to speak publicly to the NCC and UFMCC. The idea was to get scholars on both sides of the issue in order to have balance.

After some time had passed, NCC members of the steering committee informed us that they were able to find several suitable scholars to speak on the side of supporting a revised view of homosexuality and the Bible but could find no one who would speak on the more traditional side of the issue. We in UFMCC responded by providing several names of scholars familiar to us who are known for their traditional views on this subject. The NCC folks countered by saying that none of those "scholars" was acceptable, as they were not represented in the "guild" of Scripture scholars or did not come from the churches of the NCC.

Finally, the steering committee proceeded by asking an Old Testament and New Testament scholar to be the presenters, Drs. Robin Scroggs and Bruce Schaefer. Both Scroggs and Schaefer presented information and conclusions that support UFMCC's position on homosexuality and the Bible. Dr. Schaefer said during his presentation that today (1987), "no serious Bible scholar would make the statement that the Bible unilaterally condemns homosexuality." That was the first time I ever recall any scholar making that statement. I thought it was probably the most important outcome of the consultation. Frankly, I thought it should be front-page news. But of course it never made it to the front page or even to the back page of any newspaper, or NCC press release. Our committee was permitted to report on the consultations to the NCC Governing Board, which we did. The board received our report and our very heartfelt request that the results of these consultations, especially the biblical consultation, be published, distributed, discussed in the churches, debated, challenged and taught. The NCC then went through a painful leadership crisis, and the papers from our consultations were buried and ignored. To my knowledge, that was the first time in history that such a critical study of homosexuality and the Bible was presented and authorized at that level of Church anywhere in the world. And yet the papers and findings remain suppressed to this day. (Although one can order the primary documents from the NCC Information Office, 475 Riverside Dr., New York, New York, 10011).

The leaders of mainline denominations and seminary professors from member churches of the NCC have paid for and studied this information about homosexuality for many years. Even conservative scholars like Richard Hays from Yale (notoriously homophobic in his biblical interpretation—I don't know if he is or was in "the guild") now admit that, for instance, the story of Sodom and Gomorrah is not and never was about homosexuality.[12] Yet the vast majority of Christians in and outside the churches of the NCC still believe outdated, erroneous, homophobic biblical interpretations. The Church leadership refuses to teach what it knows. The violence and hatred perpetrated against gays and lesbians in our culture is silently—and sometimes not so silently—co-signed by the Church. Church leadership knows that teaching the truth about homosexuality and the Bible will be controversial, difficult and, at first, costly. The fear of controversy, of loss of money, of criticism from the radical right keeps the truth locked up.

I am a little more encouraged, though. Heterosexual ministers like Methodists Jimmy Creech and Gregory Dell are starting to defy the Church's homophobia boldly and openly, challenging old Biblical assumptions about homosexuality, gay marriage, etc. When heterosexuals start taking risks for our cause in the Church, start losing their jobs and their churches, the Church will change more quickly. Until person who are not gay start taking our cause seriously as a human rights cause, and suffer persecution for it, we will not "win' in the institutional church. It reminds me of the Abolitionist movement, that had to draw determined, devoted white clergy and laity, women and men, to its cause before the dominant culture started to embrace that slavery was evil.

Several years ago my friend, gay Presbyterian Chris Glaser, went undercover to an "ex-gay" conference in San Diego attended by 500 very sincere folks. Chris, in reporting about this in *Frontiers* magazine and in conversations with me, said that there were no workshops about "Homosexuality and the Bible" at this conference. Instead, there were lots of testimonies from "healed gays" and seminars in bad psychology. Nothing on the Bible? Can it be that all the published critiques of traditional views of homosexuality and the Bible are becoming more difficult to refute? Have we begun to succeed in taking all the fun out of Bible study for homophobes?

I have noticed that both in articles by folks such as Richard Hays and in street-corner debates, the *soft sell* is very in. They've stopped talking about specific Bible passages (since we have credible responses now to Sodom and Gomorrah, Leviticus, Romans, and 1 Corinthians), and they're back to using pitiful statements like "God made Adam and Eve, not Adam and Steve." Well, true, God did make Adam and Eve. Charming heterosexual role models!

One of my most challenging street-corner encounters with fundamentalists happened in West Hollywood in the mid-'90s. But first, a little background information:

In the late 1980s, I got a call from Connie Norman. Connie was a mad and brilliant transsexual earth mother to all gay and lesbian, AIDS and justice activists, especially the young ones. She was someone who knew how to call out the troops for an action or demonstration. As a wonderful writer and a Los Angeles radio personality, she was always able to get my attention.

Our first serious encounter had happened the day that six or seven AIDS activists were attempting to fast on the steps of the Federal Building in downtown Los Angeles. Unbeknownst to the fasters, the federal government had changed its policy. Individuals could no longer fast overnight on the steps of the Los Angeles Federal Building (as Reverend Troy Perry had in 1977) because the feds didn't want homeless persons sleeping on their steps! So, the fasters (fasting for the immediate release of DDI, the latest desperately needed AIDS medication) were ordered to move.

Connie was calling every organization she could. I happened to be in my office and decided to drop what I was doing and join them. When I got there, the crowd was growing. I jumped in, and Rev. Bob Lucas, Connie, and I handcuffed ourselves to the building. We waited about five hours for the feds to come and arrest us. When they finally came to get us, they took me first. Connie knelt and began praying the Lord's Prayer. I felt like she was doing it partly for me. I'll never forget how it touched me to be supported in that way.

They dragged me for a bit, and a very butch female federal agent said in a commanding voice, "Nancy, just stand up!" I was too dazed and stressed to wonder how the heck she knew my name, but not too out of it to disobey! They had run out of paddy wagons and were shoving us, handcuffed, into the backseats of patrol cars. Wayne Karr, AIDS activist and an outrageous person in his own right (who has since died of AIDS), was right behind me, not cooperating in the slightest. They had to drag him (handcuffed) all the way to the car. It was apparently too difficult to shove him right side up into the backseat. So they shoved him down with his face on the floor of the backseat and his feet in the rear window. Actually, most of his face was on my shoe. I kept asking him if he was all right. He laughingly said he preferred my foot to the floor of the patrol car!

So, when Connie called, I knew I may well be in for an adventure, and try to remember to take fine or bail money with me.

This time she told me of some goings-on Friday nights in West Hollywood. It seems that a group of fundamentalists, identifying themselves with the fundamentalist Calvary Chapel in Costa Mesa (which turned out later to be not quite true), were out late on Friday nights handing out antigay literature, pamphlets that said cruel things about people with AIDS and how God feels about them. Connie said, "It's getting pretty heavy out here, and I think the kids" ( the mostly younger gay and lesbians and AIDS activists, Queer Nation and Act Up folks) need to see some collars out here!"

So I took a couple of UFMCC members and clergy with me on Friday night at about 11:00 to a corner of West Hollywood Park. There they were. We could hear the din. There were a handful of fundamentalists surrounded by a very loud, screaming crowd of queers. Apparently this had gone on for weeks and had started out with rational discussions in normal tones. But it had really escalated by now. As we approached, Connie saw me, grabbed me and pushed me in front of the fundamentalists, saying, "Here's one of our ministers, talk to her!"

Frankly, it was hard to hear ourselves think. But we began to try to talk to them while also acting as a buffer between them and the screaming crowd.

I had to think fast about why we were there and how we were going to handle this. *Our* crowd (the queers) were so enraged and volatile that I knew someone was going to get hurt. And when that happened someone would be arrested, and they would be our someones. I knew we needed to defuse this situation and get these folks to leave the neighborhood. It was clear to me that the fundamentalist leader had some deep personal agendas that he was working out and had gotten some young idealistic fundamentalists to follow him out there to "save" these homosexuals. They felt like they were being "persecuted for Jesus' sake" by this angry crowd. I really believe they had no idea how hostile their activities were. By coming into the small neighborhood of West Hollywood—one of the only gay and lesbian-identified cities in the world, just a few square blocks of relative safety and openness—they were violating our sense of peace and safety. Safety from bigotry and insult, as well as from physical harm. The fundamentalists had invaded West Hollywood with judgment, condemnation, and pity, all "in Jesus' name"—with love!

I also surmised that a lot of the queer folks on the street were working out their issues on these fundamentalists. How many of these men and women were preachers' kids or were themselves from conservative religious backgrounds? Victims of religious abuse? Even for dedicated activists, it took a lot of commitment to be here every Friday night.

We tried to defuse things by standing between the two groups and engaging the fundamentalists. It unnerved them suddenly to have people talking to them who were not shouting, and who actually knew something about the Bible, and who had in common with them that we would say the words *God*, *Jesus*, and *Bible* without expletives attached.

I took on the leader and attempted to help him understand that Jesus never exercised his ministry in a way that made the materially or spiritually poor, the outcasts, feel *worse*. In fact, Jesus criticized the Pharisees who heaped their judgmentalism and narrow interpretation of God's law on the poor outcasts. The leader asked me if I thought the gay folks were behaving in a very *Christian* manner. I said, "No," but they weren't claiming to! And what kind of treatment had they received from so-called Christians?

By now, Richard Davis, Rev. Sandy Williams, Rev. Joseph Gilbert, and others of us had our hands full. The leader seemed more than a little shaken. He made noises like they might want to leave, and we got some one to call them a cab immediately. Then we escorted them to the main street. At one point, the leader attempted to put his hand on the shoulder of an angry young man, who screamed back at him. I took a big chance and with both hands grabbed the young man's shoulders and said, "Cool off, they're leaving." He turned to me with a look of joy and said, "How did you convince them that we are right?"

Well, of course, I hadn't done any such thing. I had only convinced them to leave—because this was not a safe or welcome place for their ministry. Freedom of speech does have its limits and responsibilities. Later the leader of the fundamentalist group tried to sue the police department and the city, saying that they had been battered in some way. I had to testify to the sheriff's department about my own observations to the contrary.

But the young man's response haunted me the most. It amazed and saddened me how much he wanted the fundamentalists to change their minds! For them to give him some kind of love, approval or validation that he hadn't gotten or wasn't getting elsewhere. I was amazed that he would be so naive as to believe that rational discourse and debate about the Bible with such folks can have any real impact. There is this hunger for acceptance and legitimacy that underlies some—but not all—of the rage I saw that night and have seen many other times. That this young man wanted validation from fundamentalists shocked me.

Also, somehow, even though we were Christian ministers, the crowd trusted us. That also amazed me. We were *their* religious queers!

The issue of the desire or need for approval from religious authorities (fundamentalist or otherwise) is a very touchy one, especially in UFMCC where we do not want to be isolated, but to be a part of the broader Christian church. It is a narrow tightrope to walk at times. I worried that just by applying for membership in the NCC we in UFMCC were giving them the power to reject us, and thus giving their evaluation of us too much legitimacy. I worried that the seemingly inevitable rejection by NCC would only deepen our self-esteem issues as a church. We had to continue to exorcise from ourselves (especially those of us who dealt closely with the NCC) our own personal demons of self-doubt, to remember that our cause was twofold: expose their homophobia, and witness the miracle of the spiritual movement occurring among our sisters and brothers in the gay and lesbian community. Gaining their approval was *not* our purpose. But it was hard, sometimes, in the midst of the battle to keep that perspective.

Part of moving toward a positive lesbian and gay interpretation of the Bible means being willing to move ahead without the approval of fundamentalists or the NCC, and without converting them! No one is going to make this effort, this reclaiming of the Bible, easy for us. Nor can we make it comfortable for them—for fundamentalists, Lutheran bishops, Presbyterian pastors, or even the Pope.

### A Catholic Encounter with Homosexuality and the Bible

In 1987, Pope John Paul II visited the United States. One of the big events was to be a worship service in a stadium in Columbia, South Carolina. This was the *Protestant* showcase service and all the leaders of the NCC, plus Southern Baptists and others were invited. All national Protestant church leaders were invited, and Rev. Troy Perry was on the list. We were never sure who made that decision in the National Conference of Catholic Bishops (what gay or gay-friendly person) but we were invited to participate in a procession of Protestant clergy into the stadium and to hear the pope preach. Despite Troy's previous negative experiences with the NCC, he just couldn't resist this. He asked me to go with him.

Now, as a lesbian pastor in a church that has its roots in the counterculture, I have an interesting history with just what is proper lesbian preacher attire! By 1987, I had gotten past the denim stage in the '70s and had since been wearing pantsuits and clergy shirts. I had even bought a more dressy suit or two to wear to the NCC meetings, mostly so that I could blend in a little better. I figured I was "different" in enough ways obvious to all of us that I didn't need to make a statement with my clothing. (Like a lesbian flannel clergy shirt or something) However, the '80s saw the revival of skirts and dresses in a big way (thanks to Ronald Reagan and the conservative wave), and this did make me feel a little awkward at

## 105

times, and pressured to dress differently. With the invitation to worship with the Pope, it seemed as good a time as any to deal with the skirt thing.

By this time I was pastor of MCC Los Angeles. Sweet, sharp-dresser Lloyd King, a member of the church, now in his 80's, gave me some money so I could dress myself. Lloyd was usually dressed in a white or tan suit with a purple tie, impeccably manicured and coiffed. I tended to roam between the men's and women's departments when I looked for dressy clothing, but this time it was women's clothing all the way! I was shocked at the prices of skirt suits and dresses since I had last bought them (probably high school). So, I took the plunge and bought a suit, with a straight skirt and hemline below my knees. My spouse Paula calls it my *nun* outfit.

Troy and I were both excited and nervous, not knowing what to expect at this event. We flew into Columbia, S.C., for an overnight. We saw no one we knew, and ate dinner together. Then I had to go to the drug store. And unfortunately I confided in him that wearing a skirt suit meant I had to wear pantyhose. And that I had not worn pantyhose in 15 years and that when I wore them last, women shaved their legs. And I just didn't think I could wear pantyhose without shaving my legs! He thought that was hilarious. And proceeded to include this in his repertoire of Fellowship folklore: *how Nancy shaved her legs for the Pope*.

Duly shorn, pantyhosed, and beskirted, I got in the car with Troy the next day as we drove to the stadium. Even in low heels, managing getting in and out of the car in heels and a straight skirt was a challenge. I kept praying that the Pope would be on time, and that I wouldn't have blisters on my feet by the time we went through the reception line.

When we got there, the rumor was that the Pope was late because there was a hurricane in Miami. We were herded into a large room, where eventually nearly all the 400 people in the procession were gathered. There were Catholics, Protestants and Eastern Orthodox, clergy from the historic black churches, women and men religious. We had vested, and then we ended up waiting for four hours in the early September South Carolina heat and humidity. Just *fabulous* for me in skirt, pantyhose, and heels. And Troy in his heaviest three-piece suit and layers of vestments.

All of our deodorants were sorely taxed. Just to add to the perspiration in the room, and to identify ourselves a little more, Troy and I wore our buttons that said, "God is greater than AIDS." People would smile, introduce themselves sweetly, squint at our buttons, and read, "God is greater than AIIIIIDS," and turn away and quickly talk to someone else. There were a few friendly NCC folks and a lot of unfriendly faces. The tension mounted as the temperature increased. I do not ever remember seeing so many police. The campus ROTC guarded us, assisted by the state police, local police, the FBI and the Pope's own secret service. It was a mad house.

Finally *he* arrived, and the procession began, some people still giving us the "how the hell did you get invited" looks. We processed in. Troy and I ended up on opposite sides of the football field, with the crowds watching above. I ended up surrounded by the Orthodox clergy, of course. As we walked in, someone unfurled a gay pride sign in the bleachers.

The service began with an opening prayer by a woman in a clerical collar. She then walked off the podium—by prior agreement, we learned. The Pope would not be on the same podium with a woman wearing a clerical collar!

Then came what was to be, for me the highlight of the event, and the star of it was the Bible.

Helen Hayes read the first lesson, from the Hebrew Scriptures. She read Ruth 1:16-17.

> But Ruth said, "Do not press me to leave you or to turn back from following you! Where you go, I will go; where you lodge, I will lodge;
> Your people shall be my people, and your God my God. Where you die, I will die; there will I be buried.
> May the Lord do thus and so to me, and more as well." (NRSV)

I was stunned. I had been sitting there thinking, "What the hell am I doing here?" This pope has not been exactly a leader in the area of justice for women, gays and lesbians! In fact, for someone so well educated who had spent his early life in the theater, he seemed the very paragon of sexual repression.

But along came Ruth and Naomi that day in South Carolina. It was like the Bible itself was speaking to me that day, reassuring me. The Bible was secretly overturning the moment, speaking for itself. The story of Ruth and Naomi was our text! It is the most profound statement of committed love between two human beings in the Bible, and it is said between two women. There was Helen Hayes, reading this beautiful statement ("Where you go I will go, where you die, I will die"), right out there in front of the Pope, God, and everybody. It was a profound victory for lesbian hermeneutics.

Then the Pope himself read from the Gospel of Mark, chapter verses 31-35.

> Then his mother and brothers came; and standing outside they sent to him and called him. A crowd was sitting around him; and they said to him, "Your mother and your brothers and sisters are outside, asking for you." And he replied, "Who are my mother and my brothers?" And looking at those who sat around him, he said, "Here are my mother and my brothers! Whoever does the will of God is my brother and sister and mother. (NRSV)

Again, the choice seemed strange. First of all, this is one of the passages where it is mentioned that Jesus has brothers and sisters. In Catholic doctrine, which teaches the immaculate conception of Mary and her perpetual virginity, Jesus is said to be without brothers and sisters. Even modern Catholic translations like the Roman Catholic-sponsored Jerusalem Bible claim that the word for brothers and sisters may also have been used to mean "cousins." No Protestant commentaries say this. Secondly, I had always seen this text as one of Jesus' harshest statements against the idea that one's biological *family* relationships should define one's identity. In fact, Jesus *redefines family as those who do the will of God!*

The Pope then proceeded to use these two texts to preach a sermon that was essentially a campaign speech for *traditional family values!* He did have a really good subtext on the cross (he was, after all, in Baptist country). But most of the sermon was consumed by the "family values" stuff. Family values from whose tradition? Whose family? Both those Bible passages *critique* any "traditional" (really, modern!) understanding of family values. The Pope essentially ignored that in his interpretation or lack thereof.

And then he blessed the children. Later I would write a short piece for *The Christian Century* about it. He blessed a couple dozen children that day, at least ten percent of whom were gay and lesbian. I was thankful that at least the Bible provided a *balance* that day, and I prayed that when those children grew up, they would be included in the pope's version of family. The Pope's sermon was so loaded with the "traditional family values" stuff that both Troy and I were expecting him to say something overtly homophobic. It never happened—and we hadn't planned what we would have done if he did. Would anyone on that big football field have taken notice —other than the FBI or the Pope's secret service?

The Pope had to rush off right away, being five or six hours behind schedule, so the promised reception line never happened. We disappointed friends back home just waiting to see us shaking hands with the Pope. Troy, in fact , had gotten phone calls all week from religious leaders (some not invited), instructing him on how to properly address the Pope as a non-Catholic, and what kind of contact you had with him when you didn't kiss his ring...We went to the reception anyway and mingled with NCC leaders and Catholic bishops. A few of the bishops were extremely solicitous and knew right away who we were. One of them was well known to be actively homosexual. We are everywhere.

### Lens of Prison and the Prisoner

Probably not until MCC L.A.'s building on Washington Blvd. in Culver City, was destroyed in the Northridge earthquake of 1994, did I really appreciate the story of Paul and Silas in prison—during an earthquake!

The Book of Acts is the story of preaching and practicing of the "unhindered gospel" (Acts: 28:31) and the increasing self-discovery of this new movement which was not really even a church as yet. Those early followers of the Way were adventurous, and totally committed to sharing the life-giving healing grace of God in Jesus Christ. They lived and died to do this.

An earthquake figures in one story of the sharing of the Gospel: Paul and Silas are in Philippi, where they have meet Lydia (seller of purple, head of her household), and started a house church. (Acts 16).

Inevitably, Paul and Silas run into opposition. A slave woman, who the Bible says was possessed of a "spirit of divination," was harassing them. All mostly offhandedly, out of annoyance, not compassion, Paul heals her in the name of Jesus. She is now in her right mind, very grateful, but useless as a "diviner."

The men who profited from her spiritual or mental illness (she was a sideshow), are not amused. They have lost the coins people tossed at this raving lunatic. She was their property and Paul and Silas interfered. Even unwittingly, Christ's servants in this story are on the side of this poor, oppressed exploited woman. They are thrown into jail, and while they are there, they sing hymns of praise to God.

And then the earthquake happens. The jailer assumes that all the prisoners have fled, and that he will be blamed. As he begins to throw himself on his sword, Paul and Silas call out to him not to harm himself, that all the prisoners are there. This act of mercy, so unexpected, unnerves the jailer, and he takes Paul and Silas home. He leaves his post, no longer fearing the authorities, he is now free, and he and his household become Christians.

Paul and Silas could afford not to flee, because, even in prison, they were already free. They didn't care whether they were in jail, or where they were. All they had to do was praise God, and enjoy God's acting and moving through them—anywhere, even in jail.

I have seen that same spirit among South African political detainees, like Simon Nkoli, who were tortured and illegally imprisoned for years fighting aparteid. Simon was also gay, and educated his fellow ANC comrades in prison, influencing their eventual pro-gay stance when freedom came and Mandella was elected. I've seen that spirit in AIDS Activists, and those struggling for peace. The joy of suffering for righteousness sake.

When Fr. Malcolm Boyd, Rabbi Denise Eger and Rev. LaPaula Turner and I were arrested during yet another AIDS protest in front of the Los Angeles County Board of Supervisors, we were taken to our respective county facilities. The men had a much worse time of it than we did. They were chained to benches for hours on end, and not permitted to go to the bathroom.

LaPaula, Denise and I arrived just in time for lunch at Sybil Brand Institute, which they served us in the holding cell. I think LaPaula and I were both aware that Denise was a little more of a novice at this than we were. I'd been in jail and had visited many women in this particular jail before. We sang songs for her and for ourselves (like Paul and Silas, I guess, though we didn't think of it at the time.)

The guards were quiet and low-key, almost not seeing us. We were fingerprinted and segregated, kept in the smaller of the holding tanks. Across the aisle, separated by bars and glass, was another, larger holding tank full of women, many of whom looked, to me, to be lesbian. I noticed all of them pointing at LaPaula, Denise and me. They saw my clergy collar. They were laughing, thinking this was cool: a bunch of preachers busted — for what?

I tried to communicate using the little sign language I knew. I smiled and joked, thinking they knew I was a lesbian. I was able to let them know we were there for an AIDS demonstration. They were all poking each other. They kept laughing until I looked at them and signed something like "I'll pray for you." One woman's face just clouded up, all angry. "Don't pray for me," she signed, folding her arms defiantly.

Suddenly I realized that she thought I meant *praying for her because she was a sinner, a bad person, not like me.* This grieved and hurt me. No, no, I signed. "I'm a lesbian, like you." (I did look around before I said this to make sure no guards would see me.) "Really?" came the response, "No shit!" She was all smiles again. "Then you *can* pray for me," she signed. Collar or no collar, I was a *sinner*, just like her.

We at MCC Los Angeles also found this story of Paul and Silas useful, especially in the face of hostile fundamentalist earthquake theologizing about the loss of our building. It became possible to see ourselves as those who could say, like Paul and Silas, "We are still here," after the earthquake! We are not going anywhere; we are still being the people of God in Los Angeles, especially for the gay, lesbian and bisexual communities, for people with AIDS, for anyone who feels judged or excluded from the people of God, especially because of their sexuality. We are still here. Not arson or persecution or vandalism or earthquakes can stop those who know the real truth: that we are citizens of God's wonderful realm whose ethic is one of unconditional love. We are still here, testifying to jailers, judges, magistrates and our fellow prisoners. We do not experience things like earthquakes as God's special judgment or favor on anyone. But simply as one more marvelous opportunity to share the good news of God's love and to practice that Way in our own city and neighborhood.

When I first joined MCC in 1972 I was very impressed by the fact that MCC from its earliest days had reached out to gays and lesbians in jails and prisons: "hard-living" people.[5] In those days (the late '60s, early '70s), homosexuals did not have the more middle/upperclass urban image we sometimes have today. We were still considered mostly pretty unmentionable and sleazy. Therefore, it was a little easier, perhaps, for us to identify with other social out casts and misfits. We had felt the terrible sting of rejection and the pain of inhospitality, and we were determined, with every breath, not to exclude anyone. We were going to welcome all people into our churches and hearts (sometimes, even if it killed us!).

We came to understand a new interpretation of God's grace, and of the Bible, and of the sin of Sodom and Gomorrah. We came to understand that this sin of Sodom was the sin of inhospitality to strangers, of violence, physical, emotional and spiritual, towards those who were different. We who had been called "sodomites" had been "sodomized" by the Church and the culture, and we couldn't bear to do it to anyone else.

In taking this stand, we found ourselves tackling the "sodomite" tendencies of some of the largest institutions in the country: the army, the prisons, the churches, the hospitals. Places others were trying to get out of, we were trying to get into! We were searching for our people.

As a *class* of people, we gays and lesbians have more familiarity than most with jails and prisons. They form a part of our history. I remember making my first visit to a lesbian bar in the "combat zone" (a street that contained a row of porno theaters, strip joints, and notorious bars) in downtown Boston in the early 1970s and having to run out the back door because a police raid was happening. Every now and then the police would just rush in the front door of a gay bar and begin rounding everyone up, busting the heads of those who resisted (and the heads of some who didn't). It was during just such a raid that someone said to Troy Perry (in 1968) that surely God *couldn't* love us. It was this statement that propelled Troy into actually holding the first MCC service.

I pastored an MCC church in Worcester, Massachusetts, in the 1970s. After raids at the one gay bar in town (the Ports O' Call on South Main Street), my partner and I would rush to the police station. At the desk there was a TV monitor, where we watched the police beating young adults, even kids in their teens, while dragging them to their cells. We had to keep our mouths shut while we watched or risk getting beaten and jailed ourselves. If that happened, there would have been no one to come for us. So we watched, took badge numbers, times, and dates, while desk sergeants grumbled about our presence.

Sometimes if there was a scuffle at the bar or a problem in the making, we would receive a call and race down to the bar trying to intervene before the police arrived. More often than not the police would just show up for a "surprise visit," and the very sight of them would set off a chain reaction that resulted in arrests and beatings. We then reported these beatings to the Human Rights Commission, who listened empathetically, sometimes even held hearings, and usually did nothing.

While I was pastor of MCC Detroit, we formed a prison ministry team. This included a group of people (mostly lesbians) who began corresponding with inmates in Jackson State Prison, 80 miles from Detroit. Early on in the correspondence we learned of a lesbian prison inmate in DEHOCO (Detroit House of Correction, a women's state facility that I believe no longer exists) who wanted contact with MCC. I let that information sit on my desk for a few weeks, then finally got around to writing to her. The envelope came back several weeks later, stamped DECEASED. I remember how devastated I felt, holding that unopened envelope in my hands. They had a *preprinted stamp* saying "DECEASED"! This gave me a clue about how often this had to be communicated to the family and friends of those in prison. I was never able to establish another contact with lesbians in jail or prison while I lived in Detroit.

In 1982, in Los Angeles, a group of women in MCC churches in the area formed a women's prison ministry. We knew no women in prison, although a few members of MCC Los Angeles had actually joined MCC while they were in prison in the 1970s through a jail ministry at Sybil Brand (the Los Angeles women's county jail, which also houses federal prisoners). That ministry and its leaders were no longer around.

Three of us prayed for some kind of opportunity. Two weeks later, the lover of a friend of mine ended up in jail at Sybil Brand. My friend was not amused that I saw this as an answer to prayer! She was much too frightened to have me visit (and thus be identified as a lesbian), but she met a woman who was willing. I think I first visited her the way that family and friends do, standing in line outside sometimes for hours until they call your person's number. Later I would go through the process of certifying my credentials with the county so that I could visit these women as their pastor, meaning I could bypass the line and meet more privately in the "attorney room."

The word spread, and several of us on the team began visiting women on a regular basis, to the dismay of the fundamentalist women's chaplain at Sybil Brand.

We also learned a great deal from the woman who was the president of the group called Friends Outside, an advocacy organization for women in prison: Joyce Ride, mother of Sally Ride. (Her business card actually says, "Mother of the First Woman Astronaut.") Joyce knew all the ins and

113

outs of these places and how to help us deal with an institution that didn't want us to be there.

At Sybil Brand Institute, and the California Institute for Women I learned the very disturbing fact that for many of the thousands of women or so warehoused in those facilities (built for much smaller populations), prison is the safest and in some ways the best place they have ever lived. And it is not a safe or comfortable place. It is prison. In prison, these women have food and a bed (sometimes in the gymnasium without enough toilets). They have the same substandard medical care afforded to all people who are poor in the United States, only their choices are more limited. Sometimes, as recently documented in our state, they are sexually exploited by male guards.

I remember the stories of "Doctor No-Touch." He was the only physician who would actually come into one of the state facilities we visited on a regular basis. He was their primary-care physician. Apparently, some time earlier in his illustrious career, this doctor had been accused of improperly touching the women prisoners. His solution (or the state's?) was for him *never to touch the women.* In fact, he stood at least three feet away from them while he spoke to or *examined*(!) them.

Prison doctors come in only two types: those who really also want to be social workers, who are idealistic, and who generally don't last long; and the other kind—the incompetent, negligent, and sadistic.

The same can often be said of prison chaplains. As hard as the regimentation is and the various forms of humiliation, there is a kind of community in many of these prisons, especially where women have long stays. Women may be able to form actual friendships. They are not controlled, abused, or exploited by their male family members, lovers, friends or pimps. Lesbians in particular often find themselves in positions of leadership, excelling in an all-female community, not competing with men or having to combat as much homophobia. I saw lesbians who for the first time in their lives felt some self-esteem, some sense of success (in work, schools, or just socially) in prison in ways they could not feel successful *outside.*

This, of course, is a major cause of recidivism. I met women who committed crimes in order to get back into prison to be with lovers or friends. Who, when they left prison, were leaving the only home they had ever known to be anything remotely like a home, where there was some safety from violence (not totally, by any means), lots of rules (boundaries), a pretty clear system of rewards and punishments, and the possibility of intimacy. For most of these women, leaving was like trying to catch a speeding train, like leaving home without a safe place to go. One solution would be to make prison more unattractive, less safe, as many have suggested. How bad would it have to be, I wonder, to be less safe than the *outside*?

It was really hard for me to take in this lesson: that prison, with the boredom, the regimentation, the arbitrariness of the discipline at times, the negligent medical care, the bad food, the limited opportunities (women get much less of the percentage of funds for job training, rehabilitation, and education in the California prison system than do men), the overcrowding, the shame attached, the fact that they often lost their children—even with all this, prison was an *improvement* in their lives! For some it was the only positive attention and support they ever got from *anyone* in authority; the only real education that they got. As Rev. Jesse Jackson says, "Poor people in this country get first class (well, sometimes!) prisons, and second class schools."

Over and over again, as we prepared to welcome women and to be a part of their "program" as they tried to reestablish a life outside of prison and outside of the environment that had led them to prison in the first place, we ran into this. They were lonely and afraid, and it took money and volunteers to help them make it on the outside. Some had babies or children to care for as soon as they got out, had no place to live, and only 200 dollars. Usually, if they made it past the first two weeks, I began to have a little hope. I watched them try, and try hard, and then give up and go back. They'd go back exhausted and defeated.

The lesbian lifers always fascinated me. The ones I met, of course, were a select group—those who were motivated to come and be part of a lesbian-identified church in the place they might very well spend the rest of their lives. These women did not come primarily because we could help them when they got out. They were there to make life better on the inside for themselves and others. There was a kind of freedom among the lifers. Somehow, this boundary of time and space helped them relax. They had a place finally to be who they were, in a fundamental sense. This final, very hard reality of lifelong imprisonment freed them in a way. They were the ones who gave MCC inside the walls the name "Free-Spirit MCC."

Some of these women were very admired by the others and given affectionate nicknames. They were available for spiritual and emotional support to the other women. They oriented them. They were the ones the others looked to, to see if they thought we from MCC on the outside were OK. We had to prove ourselves to these women first. They also always displayed to me this tremendous kindness and openness.

### Who Preaches in Prisons?

Protestant religious ministries in jails and prisons do tend to be dominated by fundamentalists. They are our primary "competition" for the women's hearts and minds. This, I believe, is true for several reasons. For the most part, mainline Protestants have simply written off people in jail or prison—for class reasons, primarily, and because their racial group (white) is under-represented among prison populations. More poor and working-class people and people of color (even if they now have jobs and money) have relatives or friends who are, or have been, in jail or prison. Therefore, the churches that reach out to and serve those ethnic groups and classes will tend to be involved in jail and prison work.

This became especially apparent to me after I began pastoring at MCC Los Angeles. Our church is about 40 percent people of color. On an average of at least once a week I hear about family members or close friends who get shot, stabbed, raped, sent to jail or prison, who are returning from jail or prison, getting out of the hospital from a gang fight, or who get killed in a drive-by shooting. I would guess that 80 percent of the time it is people of color who tell me these stories. Members of our congregation who love each other and try to work together, especially in the gay community, live and sometimes work in different worlds, with different dangers and pressures.

Sometimes it's like we live in different cities that only occasionally (like during the riots or earthquakes) get to touch or see each other's worlds.

Because political conservatism or an "apolitical" stance (the same thing!) makes these religious groups less threatening to the status quo of the criminal justice system (especially jails and prisons), fundamentalists are much more welcome in such institutions by the authorities. They are less likely to question either the prison's rules or the officials themselves, and, in a sense, are seen as working hand in hand with the institution to control the prisoners.

Finally, fundamentalist theology is also well suited to this purpose. It works entirely on an individualistic framework. The focus is on the individual's sinfulness and the need for salvation. It feeds on guilt and shame and seeks to help the person control themselves, using the fear of eternal punishment and the desire for eternal reward. It is well suited to the prison context and philosophy. It has simple, straightforward answers for someone whose life is in ruins, who feels desperate, lost and hopeless. It also helps them to stop focusing on the frustrations of this life, of their present circumstances, or on their experiences of injustice or oppression: It's all their fault, and God will forgive them (if they behave from now on and keep quiet), and things will improve in the next life. Nothing else is important.

What happens to gays and lesbians in jail or prison is that they are not only losers in this life but in the next life as well! They are often harangued from the pulpits of these institutions as the worst of sinners. The fundamentalists (and Catholics, secondarily) are practically given a franchise on prison ministries and are free to preach their homophobic gospel without interference from the government, which builds and maintains these institutions with our tax money (including gay and lesbian tax money). Some of the ministries are privately funded, but there are state-funded chaplaincies that are sometimes extremely homophobic.

One major exception to this practice has been the presence of a paid (by the state) MCC chaplain at Vacaville, California—because they have so many prisoners with AIDS and HIV, and MCC clergy have more experience with AIDS than anyone else. Our presence at Vacaville is a profound breakthrough.

Kenneth was 17 when he entered Jackson State Prison in Michigan, a poor, biracial, effeminate gay man (adolescent). He had killed someone in a drug- and gang-related context. He was still in the first few years of his life sentence when I met him. He was the first gay prisoner who ever wrote to me. Somehow he had gotten hold of a regional gay publication that had mentioned me and MCC Detroit.

I knew Kenneth for nine years. Then they moved him to another prison and I lost track of him, I'm sorry to say. It was so hard to believe. This bright, engaging, spiritual young man, his life trashed so early by a tragic series of events. Not that Kenneth ever pretended to be innocent or anything other than who and what he was. He was refreshingly honest. Almost instantly, he grasped the message of UFMCC, a church for all people with a special outreach to the gay and lesbian community. Behind the stale walls of Jackson State Prison, he breathed us in, our willingness to know him, to love him and his friends. He knew his cellmates and fellow gay prisoners needed a nonjudgmental, inclusive, compassionate perspective on the Bible and homosexuality, on God and the Church of Jesus Christ. He was a leader, handsome, energetic and passionate about what he believed.

Kenneth always talked nonstop when we met. He was an organizer, and the prison hated that. But he was smart and overly polite; sometimes he reminded me of a black drag queen version of Eddie Haskell, from the 1950's television show *Leave It to Beaver*. He *really* irritated the authorities and entertained us! He knew how to get things done. He got as many as 80 or 90 prisoners to sign a petition to have MCC come inside the walls of Jackson State Prison. He didn't discriminate either—he talked his Muslim friends into signing as well! We would coach Kenneth at our bimonthly meetings, fitting in lessons about homosexuality and the Bible, teaching about UFMCC, our beliefs. He would take these back inside and weekly send us more names of people to visit while we were there.

Our trip to Jackson got more involved; four or five of us would go and spend a whole Saturday visiting these gay men. Mostly lesbians went on these excursions. There we were, four or five white lesbians visiting mostly men of color who were also gay. That confused the authorities at the prison terribly. They couldn't figure it out. What was this all about? Why were we visiting these men? What were our perverted or sinister motives? Somehow they just didn't buy the church thing. We must be on some kind of weird sex trip. They could never believe that we believed we had anything in common with these guys—many of them "dangerous criminals."

They could never believe that to us these men were brothers—brothers in Christ and gay brothers. We saw ourselves in them. We saw in their prisons our own prisons, we saw their real and coming freedom as our freedom too.

We had a common foe as well—a ruthless symbol of the racism and homophobia that kill and ruin so many lives: Jackson State Prison, which prides itself on being the "largest walled prison in the world." Every week we were fighting the officials, the fundamentalist chaplains, the guards, and the terrible self-images of these men, their despair, their grief, their fears. We touched them when permitted, we prayed for them, we even eventually found homes for some of them who made it out. Mostly, we told them over and over again that God did not hate them or us for being gay and that their lives had meaning, purpose, and value to us and to God. Sometimes I think we should have prayed for an earthquake like Paul and Silas experienced!

They petitioned to hold MCC worship services in the prison, and the request was denied. Having won a similar suit in the state of California just two years before, we felt very excited about our prospects. Meanwhile, we kept up our visitation schedule and correspondence with these men. We also petitioned for the right to serve them Holy Communion, and were again denied.

We spent nine years and thousands of dollars in state and federal court while the state stuck to its story that we couldn't hold these services because the inmates who wanted to attend would be endangered. The state did not think it should be required to *prove* that abridging their constitutional right to freedom of religion was necessitated for security reasons. None of the 80 or so gay men who asked for those services believed that the other men would attempt to hurt them if they went to MCC services. But the state insisted that the reason it wanted to keep us out was for the safety of the prisoners, gay or straight, who wanted to attend MCC. We even argued that if they thought there would be a problem, why didn't they put on a few extra guards and just test out their theory for a few weeks?

We lost our final appeal in federal court, which supported the prison's claim that the anticipated "violence" that would occur if MCC held services there was enough of a reason to keep us out. Violence that none of the petitioners anticipated or were afraid of facing. By the time the last appeal was heard nine years later, I had left MCC Detroit and was working for MCC in California. The appeals court did rule that we could serve communion, under close scrutiny, to five prisoners at a time in a small office just off the visiting room.

The last time I saw Kenneth was in that room. For the first and only time in Jackson State Prison, I consecrated communion with these men, and we shared communion MCC style. Two of the men had never received communion in their lives. Kenneth had been Catholic, and the other man was Baptist. One was a Muslim who felt his belief in Jesus as a Muslim should not exclude him from this hard-won sacrament. So I explained communion first, then consecrated. I asked Kenneth to serve me, and that was almost too much for him. I remember how his voice broke and his hands shook as he served me. Nine years he had devoted to this moment, this small victory, this holiest of communions. I left to catch my plane to California, but I will always feel like I left a part of my heart in that room.

Kenneth would hold small meetings of MCC on the yard, in the dining area, wherever the men could congregate and converse unmolested. He read the MCC bylaws carefully and noticed that we ask each church to take an offering each Sunday and forward ten percent to the headquarters. Kenneth took this obligation very seriously and was deeply troubled because the men were not permitted to carry cash on their person or to send cash anywhere. So we worked out a compromise that he suggested. A lot of the men whom Kenneth evangelized were drag queens, only some of whom could manage to buy or get hold of makeup (I have *no* idea how). And for the "butch" guys, cigarettes were always in demand. So, Kenneth took up collections of makeup and cigarettes, which he distributed to the less fortunate among them and even managed to get to those who were in solitary confinement. Sometimes the collections were so generous he hardly had space in his cell to hide it all!

He was still bothered occasionally by the dilemma of how to tithe ten percent to headquarters, but we just kept telling him that he was doing the right thing, and that they were a wonderful example. Theirs was a powerful new twist on Jesus' story of the "widow's mite": two cigarettes and half a used lipstick—a powerful illustration of the doxology sung in so many churches every Sunday: "We give Thee but Thine own, what e'er the gift may be. All that we have is Thine alone, a trust, O Lord, from Thee."

### Lens of our Hard-Living Brothers and Sisters

In the early days of gay and lesbian liberation, I came out in the city of Boston. In 1972 there was only one lesbian bar in Boston, and it was located in the "combat zone," an area of several blocks in downtown Boston that used to house porno theaters, nightclubs, strip joints, leather bars and gay bars. I've been told it was called the combat zone because MPs patrolled the area during World War II to protect GIs on weekend passes.

There was a constant turf war among the city, police, various Mafia interests, and "legitimate" business interests. But the weapons of the war were sex and drugs. And the *victims* were the patrons and providers, the sexual outlaws, the young and restless, the old and frustrated, the lost and lonely, the adventurous.

Jacques's was a notorious place that had a heterosexual prostitute bar in front, with a "lesbian room" with a pool table in the back, and a leather bar in the basement. I was 22, just out of the closet, and had only been to one other gay bar in my life. (I'd been to 42nd Street in New York, but only in the daytime!) I was in seminary at the time and had just barely found UFMCC. I was curious about this lesbian bar. So I went there, twice.

I remember trying not to dress too much like a tourist or college student. I felt shy and totally out of place walking by the older women prostitutes perched on bar stools in the front corridor. I remember wanting to look at them and wanting to avoid looking at them all at the same time. Both times I was too afraid to descend to the leather bar downstairs. I didn't really understand what that "scene" was about. The first time my experience in the lesbian "area" at Jacques's was OK, no big deal. Tough looking middle-aged lesbians competed good-naturedly at the pool table. I nursed a beer for about an hour and went home grateful to have gone unnoticed.

The next time I went, about half an hour into my sojourn, beer bottles started flying across the room, and the next thing I knew we could hear sirens and police entering the front door, where the prostitutes perched. There was a mad dash for the back door as women vaulted over the pool table and knocked over furniture to get out. As we were trying to leave, we literally ran into guys in leather, as well as some drag queens, who were rushing up and out of the basement. Jacques's was closed down soon after.

Years later I would sit with the older lesbians at the new lesbian owned, non-Mafia bar called the Saints. These older dykes loved to entertain us with stories about the "good old days" at Jacques's and other combat-zone clubs. They wore their scars like badges of courage! They told how the cops came to know them by name after a while, sometimes letting them crawl voluntarily into the paddy wagons without the customary beatings on backs, legs and heads. Sometimes they were so drunk and disorderly they reasoned that they kind of deserved the treatment they got. They loved to play "top this," about their experiences of danger and violence, how they got away with flipping the finger at life, the cops and God. Defiantly queer, they recounted rituals of cross-dressing, drinking, posturing, raids and cops and jail—all lived within the parameters of having to go to work or being in the closet to some degree. Secrets, danger, defiance, shame and submission—all the elements of queer life, pre-Stonewall.

The first stripper I ever met, I met at church. Her stage name was "Frosty Winters." She was a headliner at the Two O'clock Club in that same Combat Zone of Boston. Her name came from her act. Apparently in a certain lighting her skin had a somewhat green-gray-mint tinge. She built her act around this physical "special effect." And she was a lesbian. Lots of the women who stripped for a living were bisexuals or lesbians. They had a private life *on the side*, usually with a butch who often resented like hell that their "femme" stripped for men or "turned tricks."

Frosty and her lover, Claire, found MCC Boston in the first few weeks of our existence there in 1972. They had first heard of UFMCC while living in Florida (a lot of strippers worked Florida clubs in the winter). Claire, though butch by most standards, had also been heterosexually married, had five older kids (none of whom were with her) and a brand new baby boy. Claire contacted the church because she wanted Eric to be baptized. She was the first lesbian mother I ever met.

I visited Frosty and Claire in their little apartment in the South End of Boston. I have to admit, I was fascinated by Frosty and her career, and this was probably the reason I checked out the combat zone in the first place. I was also doing "missionary work," dropping off church ads and cards in the clubs and in the gay section of the porno shops. (There were no gay newspapers or organizations or coffeehouses to take them to!)

Frosty and Claire were warm and hospitable to me. I never told any one how old I was in those days because I thought I was probably too young to be pastoring. I worried about my credibility. I suspect they knew anyway, but they were sweet to me and treated me just like I was an adult and knew what I was doing.

Eric was my first baptism. He was an adorable six-month-old, a blond, healthy baby. It thrilled me to touch him with the water, to hold him in my arms, to welcome him to the people of God who called themselves MCC Boston, meeting at the Arlington Street Unitarian Church.

Two weeks after Eric's baptism, I got a late night call from Claire.

Rev. Nancy Wilson

She was hysterical , and sounded drunk. Frosty was *moving out*, leaving her. Could I come over right now? I put on my clerical collar and took the bus to the South End, enduring the stares of all who had never seen a woman in a collar (or in a collar and a blue jean jacket).

When I got there, it was quite a scene. Frosty, it turns out, had an expensive heroin habit, and Claire was tired of it. Frosty didn't was to get clean, be lectured or controlled. Claire was worried about Frosty's dealer, and the danger to them and the baby. Wearing dark glasses, and looking like hell, Frosty was leaving with her bags, hailing a cab. She gave me that, "Sorry, kid!" look.

Claire was quite drunk, and crying (as was the baby). And then I noticed the gun. She started to threaten to kill herself with it, and raced out of the house. I followed her into a courtyard. I grabbed her and spun her around, at which point she shoved the gun in my stomach and said, "if you try to stop me I'll blow you away!"

Now, I had never seen a real handgun. I'd seen my grandfather's rifles, mostly sitting high up on a gun rack at the farm. But I'd never seen anything but a toy handgun.

This was one of those "pastoral" moments that neither the Religion Department at Allegheny College, nor my six weeks of seminary thus far had prepared me for. There was no time for "theological reflection" (unless you count the prayer that went something like "Oh shit.") There was no time to really consider my options. I think I did believe that if I let her go, she would shoot herself, accidentally or on purpose. For some strange reason (I knew she had been a Catholic), I didn't believe she would really shoot me. Of course, this could simply have been denial! No time to sort that out, however...I mustered up all the "priestly authority" I could manage and said sternly and, I hoped, convincingly, "Give me that gun!"

She did. She just handed me the gun. Now, I'd never *held* a real gun either, and when its heaviness landed in the palm of my hand, and I felt the cold of the steel, It began to dawn on me what had happened, and nearly happened. My knees got wobbly. Claire must have sensed this (and seen the blood draining from my face), and proceeded to help me into the house. She was also starting to enter the weepy phase of her drunkenness. So we sat in the apartment, the gun underneath my jacket next to me on the couch, as I held Claire while she cried. And the baby was crying, too.

There was no manual for this. I left my home address and phone number on the kitchen table, covered the sleeping Claire with a blanket, took the gun, Eric, a few diapers, and a bottle, and caught the bus home. In those days, it would not have occurred to me to call the police or child welfare services—they would have been so homophobic, and Claire would have immediately lost her son.

Claire got sober for a while, but eventually drank again and lost Eric to the foster care system. Years later Claire caught up with me, when she got sober again, and she told me that Eric had graduated from high school and was in touch with her again.

A lot of my ministry, and the ministry of UFMCC over the years has been to gay/lesbian/bisexual families in distress. Sometimes, just like in all families, adults who can hardly manage to take care of themselves are trying to raise and take care of children. UFMCC churches often function as all large extended families do—they help celebrate victories and bail each other out in crises. The crises of gay and lesbian families are often exacerbated by all the self-esteem challenges associated with coming out; and with trying to become whole and healthy, in our lesbian and gay bodies, minds and spirits.

# Chapter Four—Equal to Angels

Throughout history and in many places in the world today, gay and lesbian people have been demonized. As documented in previous chapters, the concept of homosexuality (and homosexuals) represents for many people the often unconscious collective sexual fears and fantasies of the heterosexual majority. We have been lied about, projected onto, and made to bear the burden of a sexually phobic and sexually obsessed culture. It is particularly the radical religious right (in various religions, not only Christianity) that has demonized us. And of course gay and lesbian people have had to struggle to overcome both the internal and external effects of this process.

A few years ago, my partner, her mother, and I were driving to visit friends in Los Angeles. Paula's mother was relating the latest homophobic comment she had heard in her small Michigan hometown. One of Paula's now ancient elementary school teachers is a member of Paula's mother's church. Somehow the subject of *those people* came up, and "Mrs. Smith" (not her real name!) said, "Well, they're all heathens, you know!" "Heathens." Paula's mother said it made her speechless. Her daughter a *heathen*? What does this term mean in this new millennium? What images does that evoke? Words like *heathen* and *pagan* evoke racist, sexist images—white, male, oppressive Christian missionary stereotypes. This is more than ignorance; it's more mean-spirited than that. Gays and lesbians are sort of the ultimate *other* lurking heathenishly by schoolyards, or in public rest rooms, or sleazy bars, or.... You can fill in the blank.

A lesbian I know was a participant in a support group for women of her culture and race who were surviving with breast cancer. She was very out of the closet in her personal and professional life, but in the few weeks she'd been attending, the subject of sexuality or partners had not come up. Two days before Janice's surgery, a woman in the group challenged

Janice about the fact that she is lesbian and said, "I can't support you in this group if you are a lesbian." Janice was hurt, speechless, never dreaming that this would be a problem. She never returned to the support group. Being a woman of color and trying to stay alive with breast cancer was *not enough* to bring solidarity, to overcome homophobia! It was OK with this woman to turn Janice out, to cause her stress two days before surgery, for her to live *or* die without human support from other *sisters*.

So, our demonized public image made me think again about the possibility of gay and lesbian angels. I want to make it clear that I am not saying that all gay and lesbian people are angels or angelic. We gay, lesbian, and bisexual people need to see ourselves and be seen as *fully human*, neither as angels nor demons. But I do think it is helpful to consider gay and lesbian angels as a corrective.

I remember when we asked the World Council of Churches on behalf of MCC *to consider* including gay and lesbian people (who are executed and tortured in many countries just for being suspected of being gay) in their human rights agenda, in the early 1990s. We weren't asking them to support *civil rights* for gays and lesbians, or religious validation. Just *human* rights: meaning the right not to be imprisoned, tortured, exiled, or murdered simply for being homosexual. When they hesitated, hemming and hawing, whining that this was "bad timing" for the WCC (never mind the "bad timing" for those being abused and murdered!), I realized the depth of the problem once again: they're not sure we're human! Human rights seemed to them to be an unreasonable request *at this time*. It made me remember that many people still see us as a "behavior" or an "issue" to debate, not as beings in need of safety or inclusion. Talking about human rights and gay and lesbian people in the same sentence was *difficult* for them to tolerate.

In some ways the concepts of "angels" and "demons" are constructions of a perceived split in the human moral and spiritual self—the good and bad in all of us. On the other hand, the Bible and a lot of Christian (and non-Christian) theology have posited actual beings in a spiritual realm, know as demons or angels. There has been a virtual fad in recent years of speculating about the existence of such angelic beings. (Possibly a sign of millennial anxiety, reinforced by the need to sell the millennium.)

In the Bible angels are often fierce, frightening, or so well disguised that they are able to pose as ordinary humans (like the angels in Genesis 19). What I am interested in is the process of suggestion and association, not necessarily a thoroughgoing theology of angels. We probably get more of our ideas about angels from popular culture (Clarence the bumbling angel in *It's a Wonderful Life*, for instance) than from the Bible.

In Los Angeles (the City of Angels) one of the AIDS service agencies, the one that provides lunches to housebound people with AIDS, is called Project Angel Food. To those who are lying in beds of pain and weakness (sometimes with no one to visit or stay with them during the day), a person appearing at their door with a smile and a hot meal *is* an angel.

Gay men and lesbians were the ones who started most of the AIDS agencies in the United States during the first decade of the AIDS epidemic. Those organizations were built and are currently sustained by hundreds of thousands of volunteers and volunteer hours. One of the sociological realities that has made this possible is that proportionately fewer gays and lesbians are encumbered with the demands of child care and raising children. But even those who *are* have been swept into the tremendous community efforts that have cared for hundreds of thousands of ill and dying friends, lovers, neighbors and strangers. Armies of lesbian and gay angels, gay and lesbian Mother Teresas, feed, clothe, bathe, nurse, hold, hug, touch, carry and love the sick and dying men, women, and children who have AIDS.

It's not that straight people have not also been there, and done it— but *we* did *most* of it. And we've also done the praying, the memorials and funerals (sometimes when no one else would do them) and the comforting. We've done this in the face of the virulent, religiously motivated homophobia and AIDS phobia that communicate to the world, "AIDS is God's gift to the gay community." The need became overwhelming, at least in the first 15 years of AIDS, and many gay and lesbian persons with any leisure time or disposable income were pressed into service or extra giving in some way for some period of time.

For those of us in UFMCC, AIDS has dominated our local church pastoral care services and our community outreach programs for nearly two decades. Everyone who serves selflessly in our culture is deemed an "angel" in the popular mind. The term *angel*, as in "be an angel," has come simply to mean someone who will serve another not for selfish gain and who does it cheerfully, without being expected to be paid back. Somehow deeds of kindness and charity are beyond what we think we can reasonably expect of other humans.

Somehow, "be a human" doesn't conjure up the same warm, openhearted, giving image! In fact, "I'm only human" is the great excuse for letting ourselves and others down. It is the all-encompassing excuse for screwing up. What a definition of humanness!

Sometimes the concept of angels is linked to those who have died, as a description of their afterlife role. I have not found a particular biblical justification for this point of view. Mostly the Bible seems to view angels as a separate category of existence. Angels are a special species of spiritual beings, independent of humans: they are messengers from God who communicate with us from time to time but who mostly seem busy keeping God company in heaven.

Nevertheless, this popular version of the afterlife has humans living a quasi-angelic existence and sometimes includes the assumption that after death we get transformed (or recycled) as angels. It's not clear to me if this includes all people, even ordinary people (like the inept Clarence from *It's a Wonderful Life*), or only really, really good people. Also, the relationship of angelic existence to what the Church has called the "communion of saints" is not very clear. However, popular theology does not worry itself about theological *correctness*.

The concept of the communion of saints in Christian theology is the belief that those who die *in Christ* commune together eternally before the throne of God and that, from time to time, the Church experiences their collective witness and presence (Hebrews 12). We might say that this is the way in which Westerners incorporate the ancient (and, in indigenous cultures, nearly pervasive) practice of venerating (or worshiping or honoring) one's ancestors.

In fact, I remember the story of a young man in Germany who was the lover of the German-born pastor of MCC Hamburg. This young man had been a "boat person," a refugee from Vietnam. At age 11 he was rescued by Australians and eventually sent by churchpeople to Germany where he was placed in a foster home. John was gay. A Vietnamese gay man, he was now a German immigrant. His religion of origin was a Vietnamese native religion that was based on ancestor worship. He attended one of his first Christian worship services ever in London at an MCC European conference. There, at an AIDS vigil, he heard people calling out the names of those who had died of AIDS, praying for them and their families and friends, naming and mourning the losses. John, for whom English is a third language, was not sure what was happening. He whispered to his lover, a former Baptist pastor, "Are they calling on their ancestors?" It was a very logical and reasonable assumption!

Also, there was *truth* in that question. Hebrews 11 speaks of our "ancestors in faith" and what it means to remember those who die in faith as part of a heavenly community. Many of those who have died of AIDS are our *spiritual ancestors*, our particular communion of saints.

One of the things that has happened to lesbians and gay men because of AIDS and because of the virtual epidemic of breast cancer among women in the United States and among lesbians is that we have had to experience the death of dozens or even hundreds or thousands of people we have known personally or have known of, who were often our own ages, more or less. We have experienced this *selective holocaust* while the rest of the world went on with business as usual (meaning the usual, expected and also horrific losses—car accidents, other illnesses, etc.). There were times when I have greeted my friends and colleagues at UFMCC meetings, and we have spent the first five minutes saying, in small talk, not "How are you?" but a litany of "Did you hear? Did you know that James died, that Ginny is in the hospital, that Al is not expected to live the week?" People whose deaths would have had a big impact on my life ten years ago sometimes—terribly, tragically—become a footnote in my day, as in "By the way, Bob died (yesterday, last week, did I forget to tell you?)."

In December 1993 we had a very long staff meeting at MCC Los Angeles. At the end of the meeting, we were making prayer requests. I asked for prayers for our assistant pastor, Dan Mahoney, who was dying of AIDS, and for a young colleague, a student clergy, Doug Bull, who had been in a class I had taught. I mentioned that I was going to visit Doug in the hospital the next morning. My associate pastor, Lori, turned to me, put her hand on my arm, and said quietly, "Doug died this morning." I remember the shock wave—like a little electrical jolt that went through me. She thought I knew already. I didn't. Now I did. And there was the *terrible* thought that was *partially* a relief: one less hospital visit to make. Then I felt guilt. I was too late: he had left without my visit. How is his lover Bruce doing? I filed those questions in my mind and went home.

The next day I went to the Veterans Administration Hospital business office with my assistant pastor's lover, Patrick, trying to cut through red tape to get Dan into a hospice. This took nearly three hours. While I was at the hospital, my father died. I flew into my office as usual, and a volunteer said, "Your mother has called twice; she's holding on line one for you now." My mother *never* calls me at my office. I knew before I answered the phone, although, when she told me, I had to ask her to repeat it.

While I was in New York at my father's funeral, Dan Mahoney died. He had been my assistant pastor *and* dear friend for many years. At his funeral, I learned of the death of two other people whom I knew and of the critical illness of another. As Rev. Perry was in Australia, I had to fly to assist or speak at two more funeral out of town. At each one of those, I learned of the deaths of people I knew. Early in January, Dan's lover Patrick became ill, and died in March. Sometime later that month, at the funeral of a father of a close colleague and friend, I saw Bruce Bull, Doug's partner, and found out that Doug's funeral had been held the same day as my dad's. I had never even called Bruce.

It seemed finally to have happened to me—what had happened to so many of us: the body count got too high, the pile too deep. I had lost track, I couldn't keep up, I kept meaning to call Doug's lover; I think I left a message on his machine; I'm not sure I ever did. I as grateful for the opportunity to see him at person (at yet another funeral), and circle closed for a moment, but only for a moment. The lines between life and death blurred for me in this process. The less-than-totally reliable rumor mill sometimes had people dead and buried before they were hospitalized! Or it left others behind, pitifully long dead before anyone has time to notice.

Sometimes when people get ill they shut out their friends and church family. The hardest days for some of us are finally getting through to someone who tells us, "Santiago died three months ago; didn't you know?"

Lloyd was an angel, I'm sure of it. I met him through fellow angel Lew. Lew ended up at a different hospital than he usually went to, and afterward I would come to believe that it was so I could meet Lloyd.

On the AIDS ward that day at this hospital, there were a number of patients in need. Also, as usual, I was already running behind schedule, which meant I was not feeling as relaxed and attentive as I would like to be while visiting people in the hospital. I finally got *out of there* and was rushing through the lobby to the parking lot when a woman stopped me.

I must digress for a moment. Being a clergywoman and wearing a clerical collar in public is always an interesting experience—especially in lobbies, on lines, or in elevators, where someone feels compelled to make conversation. Once, in an elevator at the Veterans Administration Hospital, a young, tall, pleasant-looking man said, "Are you a minister?" (That, by the way, is the most common question. I'm not sure that any clergy*man* in a clerical collar has ever been asked that question.) Over the years I've tried to think of clever comebacks, but none of them quite matches the strangeness of the question. I think I always want to ask them why they think anyone would wear this silly outfit if she or he were *not* a clergyperson? What is it they imagine I'm doing in this shirt if I'm *not* a clergyperson? Anyway, some times, "Are you a minister/priest/clergyperson?" is the whole of the matter. But this day it also included *"because..."* (uh-oh, here we go!). At this point the young man looked furtively around in the empty elevator while also assessing just how many floors we had left in which to continue this conversation: "...because the doctors want me to give them a sperm sample to take a test, and they want me to, you know, touch myself to get the sample. I thought maybe there was *another way to get it."*

Now, as a frequent victim of people's sexual projections and unique and interesting forms of sexual harassment, I can pretty much tell which kinds of conversations are going in what directions with what motives. Even though I might have preferred this question to be the garden variety sexual come-on or harassment (a new variation on an old theme), I had the sinking feeling that he was absolutely sincere. It is strange to think that I might have preferred it to be harassment—but that's probably because then I could have just confronted it or brushed it off. I also recognized that he was developmentally disabled in some way, though this was not immediately apparent. I replied, "So, you were taught that masturbation is a sin, and the problem is that these doctors are asking you for something you were taught was wrong?" "Yes," he said, relieved that I had understood him and said some words he couldn't quite say.

Somehow, in the next few seconds, I was able to ask him if this test was really necessary and important. He said, "Yes." I asked him to consider whether he could let himself think about how God had created and loved him. Could he perhaps think that God would make an exception in this case because of his health and that God would not be angry at him if he masturbated for a really good reason? At this he broke into a smile and said, "Yes, ma'am, thank you!" and ran off the elevator.

Sadly there was no time to talk to him about God and guilt and sexuality and all that good stuff of contemporary sexual and ethical discourse! And I didn't want to give him just *my* answer. But he needed permission to think of God (and his own body) differently for the moment and to try on an alternative answer. It was a strange momentary dilemma for me. At that moment, to him, I had the authority to speak for God, as a clergyperson (perhaps a lesser type of angel) to whom he could ask a very private, vulnerable question in the confines of our temporary elevator/confessional. He related to me with a touching, childlike innocence and trust, not worrying that I would be offended, or shocked, or put off, and I guess I wasn't. I took him seriously, at his word. And I knew he simply needed to be released from a false sexual guilt, from a terrible legalistic burden: forced to choose between health and God's approval.

I've had hundreds of encounters like these, some even more "high risk." Being female and lesbian, I've probably had more than most. Women are great, wonderful, when they see me in my collar: they get excited and curious. On one airplane trip, a Baptist flight attendant couldn't stop looking at me or talking to me. She wouldn't let me get back to reading my book. Women who have always wanted a woman pastor but have never seen one before often want to confide in me or to touch me, take me home with them, replace their male pastor with me.

Ralph was an HIV-positive member of my church. His 70-year-old mother, a gospel singer in ministry with her husband for *50 years*, was getting divorced. (The husband had run off with a younger female choir member.) She was devastated, and her church family shunned her, and her male pastor *blamed* her. Divorce is always the woman's fault. Her shame and rage were overwhelming her, as well as her vulnerability—ashamed and divorced at age 70, with a son who was vulnerable, too. Her son called me and asked me to come talk with his mother. We talked for hours.

At first, she was embarrassed that she had always teased Ralph about going to "that church!" (meaning that awful gay church.) She loved being able to talk to a woman pastor, forgetting that I was a lesbian from "that church!" But, just being female made such a difference for her. She didn't feel judged by me, or shamed in my presence, or less than.

While attending a Roman Catholic seminary, I took a class with a group of older Catholic sisters, none of whom had ever even had a chance to go to college. The course was on prayer and included self esteem as part of the subject matter discussed. Sister Dorothy complained that all these years in the convent she was supposed to *obliterate* any thoughts of self, and now she was expected to account for her level of self-esteem! I fell in love with these women. And they doted on me, which simply increased my infatuation. They were so excited that I was a clergywoman. They wanted to know about my sermons, what I wore, they touched me before and after every class.

Then they invited me to lunch after class one day. They wanted to hear *all* about my church and ministry. All my internalized homophobia got stimulated. Somehow, in some corner of *my* self-esteem, I had come to rely on these women, their approval, their support. Would it continue if they knew I was a lesbian? But I couldn't dodge them or their questions anymore. So, I told them first about UFMCC (then later about me!). When I told them of our gay and lesbian outreach, Sister Elisabeth got quiet and said to Sister Dorothy, "But we were always taught that homosexuality was *wrong*, Sister!" Sister Dorothy rushed to my defense, "Listen, they lied to us about a lot of things, Sister: remember that self-esteem business?" Right on, Sister Dorothy. They did lie to us a lot, especially about our bodies, about being female or gay.

The night the sisters came and visited me at MCC Detroit was a special treat, a memory to treasure. The Catholics at MCC Detroit that night were a little traumatized at first to see eight nuns—in their habits—troop into the second row of pews in our sanctuary: they thought they were having a horrible *lapsed-Catholic nightmare*. But by the end of the evening everyone had calmed down. As an extra bonus, seeing Sister Dorothy take communion from *me* healed a lot of doubt in a lot of formerly Catholic MCCers that night.

Back to Lloyd's story. I was in the lobby, rushing as usual, dressed in my suit and clergy collar, when Lloyd's sister, Ruth, stopped me. Now when I am in a hurry, you have to be very quick and determined to stop me, and she was. She grabbed my arm, in fact, and said "What kind of clergy are you? I mean," she amended, "what kind of church are you from?"

Well, I looked at her. It was just possible that she was a lesbian. She had spotted me. So I cut to the chase; "I'm with MCC."

She grinned, "I thought so! My brother is upstairs having surgery right now. He has AIDS, and he's having a hard time. Will you see him?" I said yes, got the details, and went back the next day. (My friend Lew, by the way, was then transferred to another hospital or went home that day, his angelic mission accomplished!)

Lloyd was a little guy, strawberry blond (just like his lesbian sister—my gaydar had been right!), with a sweet Southern Illinois country accent. He poured out his heart about dying, about all his worries (ex-lovers and family members, gay and straight, leaned on him a lot) And his business (a West Hollywood drugstore) was really like a ministry to Lloyd. He loved his customers: they were more like clients or parishioners. He felt too needed, too responsible, to die.

Something happened to me when I met Lloyd. For about two years previously I had been nearly unable to cry at all. I might tear up a little, but I could not cry and certainly could not weep, even by myself. I was shut down, with all the compounded grief and anger. The part that could just spontaneously weep or tear up (which had never ever been easy for me anyway) was totally locked away. As I sat with Lloyd, this gentle, little stranger, I held his hand. He began to sob quietly, and the sight of him (I was identifying with his hyper-responsibility) made me cry. The pleasure of those tears (fogging my glasses, wetting my cheeks) was enormous. My crying did not disturb him: it seemed to help him feel not so alone. Together we cried for so many things, including ourselves.

Every time Lloyd went into the hospital, I would see him. And I would hear a little more about this man's life. After crying with him, I cried every day that week, in my car, at home. It became natural and easy to tear up in my office, at hospices and hospitals, even when I spoke or preached. I felt like I had been healed of a disability. Lloyd had helped me in that moment to reopen to my own tears.

We held his memorial service at the juice bar next door to his drug store. The place was packed with family, friends and customers. A big poster-size picture of Lloyd in a happier, healthier time dominated the room. Over and over people testified to Lloyd's kindness and generosity. How much he gave and gave away. How he saved their lives, their dignity. How he was more than a druggist—he was a friend, healer, and a brother.

Lloyd is a part of my own communion of saints. Sometimes, having lost count a long time ago, I wonder if I know more people who have died than I know ones who are *presently alive*. Sometimes the line between the world of the living and the alive and the world of the dying and the dead is very blurred for me—as if I, like so many in my community now, live in that strange borderland between the living and the dead, where people are continually crossing over. It is a mysterious and awesome place to live. You learn how true it is that death is not a moment but a series of moments, a process. And everyone does it their own way.

I have sat by the dead bodies of young dear friends, women and men, held their still-warm, gradually cooling hands. Watched their strained and pain-lined faces relax. Miraculously, tenderly they have seemed to grow younger in that twilight moment of release.

It is a great privilege to accompany them to their border crossing. It is also not what I expected to be doing in the fourth and fifth, and now sixth decades of my life. And I'm so enraged and overwhelmed at times that I want to find someone to blame: I want revenge, I want someone to pay for all this need less suffering, including, I guess, my own. Who pays for all this stolen life and stolen time, including my life and time?

And then I think of the arrogance of that thought, that complaint. Who guaranteed or guarantees anyone one minute of life? Where do I get off feeling *ripped off*—especially when I've had the privilege of loving and serving the dying? I'm not the only one, I've discovered, who has been profoundly, eternally impacted by the untimely death of dozens, even hundreds of friends, colleagues, and acquaintances. Other friends and colleagues report seeing people in public who they are sure, for an instant or longer, are friends who have long since died. Now and then I will have a powerful sensory memory of someone and then check the date: it's their birthday or the anniversary of their death.

Jean Foye was a very *human* angel. A lifelong alcoholic with "bouts" of sobriety, she knew everyone, especially Hollywood old-timers. One day she wandered sullenly into the church. She was a raging, lifelong confirmed skeptic and a poet. You can almost automatically have my heart for two reasons: make me laugh, or be an artist, any kind of artist. Jean was an artist—*and* could make me laugh! And as an alcoholic she was also a consummate *bullshit artist*. But she was also the other kind of artist, a crafter of words.

Jean took whatever art was in my preaching and let it inspire her poetry. When she died of cancer at 72 she left behind a wonderful legacy of poetry—except it was not organized.

The day I sold my car was a particularly difficult day for me. As I hurriedly emptied the glove box, a poem of Jean's fell out (she'd been dead a year already). "How did this get in here?" Then I remembered:

when she stayed for the Sunday evening services or came on an occasional Wednesday night to church, I would sometimes drop her off on my way home. Almost in lieu of carfare she would often shove a poem scrawled on an envelope or church bulletin into my hand, such as this one about the story of Jonah and the whale:

RELUCTANT PROPHET

*Both were dwellers*
*in deep places*
*(one in the dark Bowels of ships*
*and great fish and wounded pride.*
*the other in the silvery belly of the seas.)*
*Both heard God saying "GO!"*
*but the whale did*
*as he was told.*[1]

The poem left in my glove box was one I had forgotten to "cash!" It had been left unopened, uncashed for almost a year. There it was, lovely, fresh, right on time with what I needed. She was dead a whole year but still dazzling me with her gifts. Jean was a beloved if somewhat less than stellar graduate of the Alcoholism Center for Women, which is more a movement and community than a "center." But in her last few years, Jean found a faith and relationship with God that matched the passion hidden in her religious skepticism. She found her church in her community. It was just irreverent enough, just real enough and just open enough to art and irony so that she could tolerate it.

When she was dying, I was in Mexico. But the day that she died, a lay minister in our church, Woody, showed up at the hospital. Other people from church began to arrive, and the nurses were irritated and skeptical: "Who are these people?" Woody simply announced unequivocally that they were all members of Jean's family. An African-American gay man, an Asian gay man, another white lesbian and Woody. Family?! She died surrounded by those who would happily claim her as family. You *bet* they were her family. You couldn't have asked for a finer family, if a little unusual. Now from time to time, gracefully, Jean's poems pop up in all sorts of odd places in a pile of papers, in my car, in my heart and mind, like this one:

BUT NOT FORGOTTEN

*Whether or not I find the missing thing*
*It will always be*
*More than my thought of it.*
*Silvery-heavy, somewhere it winks*
*In its own small privacy*
*Playing*
*The waiting game with me*

*the real treasures do not vanish.*
*The precious loses no value*
*in the spending.*
*A piece of hope spins out*
*bright, along the dark, and is not*
*Lost in space;*
*Verity is a burning boomerang;*
*Love is out orbiting and will*
*Come home.* [2]

## Send Them

The days prior to Christmas are always very busy in any church, and that is no less true for those of us at Metropolitan Community Church. Advent is often a frenzied time, as we try to add a dimension of piety, reflection and *centeredness* to the cultural holiday bombardment. Since the industrial revolution in the West, and especially in the United States, Christian pastors seem doomed to fight this battle against commercialism, *putting Christ back into Christmas*, sometimes guilt-tripping our people as they try to walk their own tightropes of overspending, overeating, overdrinking and other holiday compulsions.

Not only that. But holidays are a time when Americans are most vulnerable to suicide.

Holiday times are a special challenge in our churches. In addition to the traditional church Christmas eve programs, musicals, plays or pageants, we often have workshops to help people beat the holiday blues. Homophobia hits particularly hard at holidays for people who are alienated from their families, or not "out." We go Christmas carolling at gay bars, sometimes in hospices, and try to provide alternative "family" events, helping people deal with their present status vis-à-vis their families and providing extra support.

Some people leave for home for the holidays and let us know they plan to come out to their families. Sometimes that's out of a strength of conviction or a need to be honest. Sometimes it occurs in the midst of coming out about HIV or AIDS. In any case, we send people off with promises of prayer, support and hugs.

We also always offer a Christmas Day Open House. We realized that many times people from MCC would go home after a Christmas Eve service to a long, lonely Christmas Day. Some people need an excuse to leave uncomfortable family scenes ("I'm needed at my church today, Mom!") or a place to hang out with food and friendly faces.

Ben Rodermond loved food. At special church occasions, like Christmas, he would always bring a treat, something sweet and fattening. His blue eyes twinkled with mischief, his ruddy complexion partially hidden by a Van Dyke beard and a waxed, old-fashioned, handlebar mustache. Soft-spoken and a little shy, he retained his distinct Dutch accent. Ben was a large, tall man who rode a motorcycle, but you instantly sensed he was a gentle, kind person.

Ben loved all kinds of good food, including Indonesian food. He went to Indonesia after World War II. Then he came to the United States, where gradually in the '50s and '60s he began to find other gay people. Ben was there in the earliest days of MCC, feeling a strong, passionate connection to the social Gospel preached by Troy Perry. Even though Ben was not a citizen at the time and was risking more than most people, he stood openly with Troy at the first demonstrations for gay rights in Los Angeles.

Ben also loved food because he knew what it was to be hungry. Ben and his sister Henny and other members of their family had hidden Jews in their home in Holland during the Nazi occupation.

To avoid being conscripted into the Nazi army, Ben went under ground for many years as a teenager. Part of the time he hid in a small attic crawl space, while his sister brought him what little food they had, along with news from the BBC. Part of the time he roamed the streets and nearly starved to death there. But he survived. He survived and eventually found friends, gay and lesbian brothers and sisters, and a spiritual home at Metropolitan Community Church of Los Angeles. He had no patience for injustice, for bigotry of any kind. And he had a permanent sweet tooth. Back to my story.

I try to schedule very little during Christmas week, just to leave room for the unexpected and to be able (while choirs are rehearsing, deacons are decorating the church, logistical problems are being resolved!) to be free to reach out beyond our church walls a little to those who are more marginalized, especially in this season. So that was how I happened to meet Michael on Christmas Eve.

We had three Christmas Eve services scheduled for that evening, two in English and one in Spanish. The bulletins were done. The church on Washington Boulevard was filled with evergreens. We prayed that it would not be too cold (as it can get in the L.A. desert climate), as our inadequate heater seemed only to *taunt* us with the hope that it might actually heat up the sanctuary.

My sermons were also done: one for the earlier crowd that included more seniors and people with young children, and one for the more lively "midnight mass" group, on their way to or from Christmas parties or family gatherings. This was one of the occasions in the year when people brought straight parents, children and family members or gay and lesbian friends who wouldn't be caught dead in church on an ordinary Sunday but for whom it was *cool* to show up on Christmas Eve.

So I had the entire day *free* on Christmas Eve, which is what I had planned. There were no last-minute emergencies and only one person in the hospital (which would be my last stop before getting to the church office later that evening).

I decided to stop by three hospices on my way into town. I have always been told by hospice and hospital staff that churches and groups visit patients (especially those without families) all during the weeks up to Christmas but that the visits come to a halt on Christmas Eve and Christmas Day. Most people, including clergy, are simply too busy on those days with their own families and church business. So it felt like my unplanned Christmas Eve and Day visits were more needed and possibly more timely. I set out to visit with a kind of quiet hopefulness, not knowing what would await me.

The first place I went was a hospice I had visited a great many times. At least half a dozen of our members had died of AIDS in this hospice. I knew many of the staff, some of whom were members of UFMCC or who had associations with us over the years. So they didn't look too surprised to see me.

It was a foggy day. The hospice was nestled in a wooded area near a park in downtown L.A. It is a small facility, with a comfortable living room and a devoted staff. This Christmas Eve, it was quiet in a kind of eerie way. When I arrived everything seemed so still. All the holiday hubbub was over before it had begun. There were no family members hanging around as there often are. No music was playing.

I asked the staff if there was anyone who needed a visit from me today. Two staff members looked at each other and communicated nonverbally. Then the nursing coordinator, a man, said, "Well, there's Michael—he's having a hard time." They related to me that they had had a Christmas party the day before. Michael was too upset and maybe too angry and ill to come out of his room. They said that Michael was physically very near death, ready to die, but he seemed anxious and afraid. They knew nothing about his religious issues. But they said, "He just can't let go." They told me he was 25 years old and had a sister.

With that little bit of information, I knocked on Michael's door and entered. Even with all the death and dying I had seen, I wasn't quite prepared for this one.

Michael was young. And maybe of average height, but he weighed only about 75 pounds. For some reason (unusual in a hospice) he had a nasal-gastric tube and tubes coming out of his mouth and abdomen. He looked a little alarmed when I entered the room. I sat down, told him I was a minister. (I thought my clerical collar might have alarmed him, as in "A clergyperson I don't recognize has come to see me—the end must be near!")

He had a notebook by his head, and he lay facing me on his left side. With his right hand he held a pencil, and I noticed a lot of scrawls on the notebook. Michael was communicating by means of this notebook, since he could not talk with the tubes in his nose and throat. His face was filled with pain and fear. He struggled to position himself so he could write on the notebook. It took quite some time for that to happen. I also realized that he was so weak that he could barely press hard enough to make a recognizable mark on the pad.

I panicked. What the hell was I doing here? I thought to myself. How are we going to communicate? Maybe I'm just frightening him *more*. I felt guilty for feeling uncomfortable. I wanted to flee from the room. I knew that only Michael, God and I would know the truth if I just left.

Whose big idea was it to come here on Christmas Eve anyway? No normal person would have chosen to be here! Was I trying to be heroic? Brave? A glutton for punishment? And now I was making this kid's suffering worse! As I thought these thoughts, Michael had finally gotten pencil in hand. "Help," he wrote. That took two minutes to write. Help. "Killing me," he wrote. Then he pulled on his gastric tube, writhing in pain. Perhaps he thinks the members of the staff here are trying to kill him.

Does he have dementia? Or is he just angry, exhausted, a little disoriented with his weakness and the medication? There was no way to know for certain. So I spoke, "Michael, I know you are in terrible pain. No one is trying to kill you, Michael." I touched his head with my hand. "You are dying, and they are trying to help you have less pain and discomfort." At that point, a tear came down his cheek. Michael struggled again to write, with agonizing slowness. He wrote again, "Help me."

I wanted to run. I have never wanted to leave a room so much in my life. Obviously I wasn't getting through, and I was frustrating him. But I touched his head again and said, "Michael, I don't know if I can help you or not. All I can do is pray for you. Do you want me to?" He seemed to nod, I wasn't sure. So I gambled and went for it. I placed both my hands on him and prayed about his fear. I prayed that he could trust God a little more. I prayed for the pain to decrease and cease, for him to be able to relax and trust God, who loved him. As I prayed, I could feel his tears on my hands. Then I felt my own tears.

We opened our eyes. He wanted to write again. This time, the writing came swiftly, mercifully. In a flourish he wrote, "This is a hospice. Christmas Eve. What are you doing here?" Great question! I had asked it myself about 20 minutes ago. I laughed a little and said, "Well, right now, Michael, I'm crying with you."

Then I noticed the Bible underneath his notebook. What church?" he wrote. "Metropolitan Community Church." He showed no sign of recognition. Imagine that—someone in Los Angeles who had never heard of UFMCC! So, as succinctly as I could, I told him *the* story. I had to assume at this point that it was likely that Michael *was* gay. I told him I was gay and about Troy Perry and UFMCC. I could see he had never heard of our ministry or about the fact that one could be gay and Christian. His eyes brimmed with tears, he even seemed to smile just a little, in between what looked like *electrical* jolts of pain. I talked a mile a minute, flooding the room with every reassurance I could manage to speak with confidence.

When I took a breath, he wrote, "Angels?" I said yes, I believed in angels and that he had the name of the greatest angel, the archangel Michael. Then he wrote, "Gay angels?"

"Gay angels?" It all came clear. Michael did not want to go any where he would not be welcome, including heaven (maybe especially). But if gay angels would accompany him, there was hope! Suddenly I remembered Ben Rodermond from Holland, who had died only three months before in the room next door to Michael's. Ben was an angel, in life and in death. I could see Ben's face suddenly, I could see him coming for Michael, bringing his little gay brother to the throne of grace, holding his hand, healing his fear. "Yes, Michael, there are gay angels: one of them died a few months ago in the next room," I said. Gay angels, what a wonderful thought; the room seemed to be filled with them. "Thank you, God," I kept saying in my heart.

Then Michael wrote again: "Send them." "Send them." He was ready now, and somehow he thought I had the ability, the authority to send the gay angels for him. So I prayed again for that very thing. Michael seemed calmer. His eyelids rested a little. Gently I touched his face and hands and kissed him good-bye.

That night at the Christmas Eve service, in our very cold sanctuary, we prayed for Michael. I called the hospice the next morning; Michael had died in the wee hours of that Christmas morning, led to his Maker, I'm sure, by Ben and his fellow gay angels.

142

# Chapter Five—Hospitality as a Queer Gift

Hospitality, as I have stated earlier, is a spiritual gift that has decidedly "queer" connections. There are profound differences among lesbians and gay men in this regard, but I think this idea works for both communities. One stereotype of gay men is that they are *fabulous* cooks and hosts of great parties. Perhaps this connection of hospitality and gays is as simple as the notion of a "queer sensibility": the love of gay men for elegance, for hospitality as an *art form*. Certainly there are gay men who are slobs or who can't cook or decorate or set a gorgeous table, but it does seem like there are a disproportionate number of them who do have a *flair* for hospitality of this kind. This has cultural and historical roots, which Judy Grahn has traced, calling us "transpeople," people of the world between genders. Our job is partly to be cultural go-betweens.

In England recently, I spoke with a gay man who had been the butler to a high-ranking member of Parliament. He told me that the royal family preferred gay men as palace servants because they were the best at providing hospitality of all kinds. Why has this queer stereotype persisted for thousands of years? Saying all this always means walking a narrow tightrope: speaking of gayness in essentialist terms can simply reinforce stereotypes. Even *neutral* or *positive* stereotypes can be used in politically dangerous ways.

When I think of lesbians and lesbian culture, I think of potlucks and an easy flow of work, preparation, food and home, sex and friends. For lesbians, hospitality is hardly ever *formal*. It is fluid, communal and easy, with everyone pitching in and not a lot of ownership of the "product." Also, it may be characterized by permeable boundaries that include parents and children and other family members, as well as bisexuals and men.

Perhaps the experience of having been left out or put out of our homes and families (even if we later reconcile with them and heal the rift) makes us more willing and open to inviting and accepting each other into our homes and living rooms and kitchens and, sometimes, bedrooms. Perhaps our neediness or loneliness has made us almost "promiscuous" in our desire to provide hospitality. Being shut out has made us want to *include* with a vengeance.

I have a collection of particular holiday memories from the first few years after Paula and I arrived in California. In the early '80s, the second year we lived in Los Angeles, we rented a fairly large house, which we could afford because we had a roommate at the time. It was Thanksgiving, the year of the U.S. Cuban refugee resettlement. UFMCC churches got involved with resettling hundreds of gay and lesbian Cuban refugees. One of Paula's former students was stationed nearby in the marines and was too far from home to go back for the holiday. We invited ten or so friends, the student, my cousin Lin (who ran for governor of New Hampshire on the Libertarian ticket), the UFMCC pastor who was the chaplain for the refugees, about five refugees and some others whom I've forgotten. Most of these folks were gay or lesbian but not all.

Every day of the week before, Paula and I would find out that we had each separately invited someone else. I think there were 35 or so people there. We actually managed to seat everyone in two rooms and at tables outside (this is Thanksgiving in California). I cooked the turkeys and basic vegetables, others brought their own dishes. The Cubans (mostly drag queens and one lesbian) experienced their first traditional (hah!) U.S. Thanksgiving, which included stuffed artichokes, Mexican lasagna, a California fruit salad, a few Asian dishes, turkey and dressing.

Other years we'd have family members of the people I had pastored who had died of AIDS. For most holidays over the last eight or ten years, someone with AIDS or HIV or who was recently bereaved (that's most of us) has been at our table. It's just a fact of life.

Each holiday has produced its own one-time-only extended family dujour. This is not a *hobby*. It is a way of living and being. It is an adventure, and it has a lot to do with being lesbian. It has everything to do with how we view life and relationship, with our own emerging values. It has to do with our own (for better or worse) family histories, how we both react in opposition to them, and how we sometimes unconsciously recreate them. It has to do with a belief that our home, our time, our table, our resources, our skills, our affection and capacity to live are to be *shared*. The sharing should support, nourish, and enrich others and ourselves, maybe for a day or maybe for years.

Many lesbians and gay men consciously create environments of hospitality in their homes or organizations. They do this as a gift, a way of life. And I don't mean that straight people don't do this. But there is some thing, perhaps, about being "unhinged" from the conventional family constructs that opens up the opportunities, the desire both to deconstruct and to reconstruct this aspect of our lives.

In fact, these days, as straight people have to deal with in-laws from more than one marriage, or divorced parents have to develop a holiday "schedule" with their kids their families get more complicated, they begin to resemble gay and lesbian families more and more. A nephew of ours married recently, and he and his new wife had nine parents and step-parents present at their wedding! We began imagining their future conflicts at holidays, and how they were going to identify each grandparent for their children, should they have any.

### Hospitality as a Central Biblical Ethic

Hospitality was essential in a desert culture, especially a nomadic one. In biblical times if you traveled anywhere in the Near East, you had to depend on the kindness of strangers and acquaintances alike. You had to treat the sojourner well because you might need to depend on someone yourself in the future. There was a common appreciation of the true vulnerability, the fragility of life in a desert climate. It was not a moral choice to be inhospitable. To do so was to violate the deepest commitment to being human and in community.

This is one of the reasons the story of Sodom and Gomorrah is recorded in the Bible. This is a story about the abuse of strangers who required hospitality. Sexual abuse of anyone—stranger, friend, or family member—is the grossest kind of inhospitality. Unfortunately, in our day sexual abuse is rampant. It is a sign of the deterioration of ethical human community. It is not primarily a "homosexual problem." It is a human problem. It results from the alienation from our own bodies and from the bodies of others.

Jesus came from a heritage of desert hospitality. As a person who during his ministry was without a permanent home of his own, he depended on the hospitality of others to survive.

Jesus knew what it was to give and receive hospitality. He knew how to be a guest. People were always inviting him to dinner! He almost never cooked; maybe that wasn't his gift, and he knew it. Perhaps others cooked for him because he knew how to appreciate good cooking. Also, he was probably a wonderful conversationalist. He brought interesting people with him to dinner and ate in all kinds of elaborate and humble settings. Dinner and table fellowship were always an excuse to talk about his passion—the nature of God and God's love, the way to live in harmony with neighbors.

He was vulnerable as a guest, dependent on the kindness of others for food and drink and presumably often a place to sleep, if not actually a bed. He probably had to deal with eating food that wasn't at its best and with accommodations that were less than adequate. He had to put up with attitudes—those who didn't like the men and women he chose to spend time with.

But Jesus was not only a guest. He also provided his own kind of hospitality. He opened himself, his heart, his body. He invited people to question him, to touch him. And they did. He invited them to test him, to see if his words were matched by his deeds. He even invited them to challenge and criticize him. Which they did.

**The Fear of Strangers**

We live in a culture that is riddled with the fear of strangers. And for good reason. Unlike in Jesus' culture, we do not feel we have any obligation to strangers. Strangers are not potential neighbors. They are potential murderers, robbers, rapists. We do not see ourselves as strangers, even when we are. Strangers are a nuisance, are dangerous.

I remember my father telling the story of seeing a car broken down by the side of the road. A woman was alone in the car, which was disabled by a flat tire. It was winter. My father spoke to her through her closed window and offered to fix her tire if she would let him in the trunk. She was obviously afraid of him. She opened her window just a crack and put the keys through (apparently not realizing that he could then have opened her door with those very keys if he had wanted to!). He fixed her tire, patiently pushed her keys through the crack in the window, and sent her on her way. Then his own car wouldn't start. No one stopped to help him, and he had to walk to the nearest gas station to get help. He always laughed at the irony of this story, but he never said that he would not stop to help someone again.

We come into the world, spending our first nine months inside another's body. Dependent on another's hospitality. Is our sexuality really partially a longing to renew that kind of intimate interdependence, that first experience of living inside another, safe and welcomed (perhaps)? How does that experience shape our sexuality, and in what way?

But all children arrive as strangers. These are strangers that we are mostly not afraid of because they are so small. But some new parents are very afraid of the demands, the needs, the reality of this new, strange little life. We cannot assume we know them.

This is a terrible contradiction for the church, which can only grow by welcoming strangers week after week. How do we shift from all that suspicion of strangers to becoming warm and welcoming? All week long, strangers call our churches for information, directions, counselling, prayer, help. At our church, MCC L.A., they call from all over the world. Strangers are our mainstay, our reason for being.

I remember two men who called, desperate, because when a friends died, they called a "community church," located in West Hollywood (not an MCC), who were terribly cold to them. The church said they didn't let "strangers" use their church. We not only let them use our church, but we let them use it for free. We helped them set up and clean up and provided greeters to assist them.

UFMCC pastors, and all clergy, to some degree, have to wrestle with these issues. We to be sensible, but we have to take chances meeting strangers. Many of us remember that Rev. Virgil Scott, of MCC Stockton, California, left his home to meet a stranger who called the church seeking help. Virgil wound up brutally stabbed and murdered and left in the trunk of a car.

I've gone to homes, alone, of people who were dying. And strangers come to my office every day, wanting to be married, or have their baby baptized, or find out how to be gay or lesbian and Christian.

Inviting strangers into our circles of friendship and love and acceptance is what a healthy, open church experience is all about. Yet this is so counter to everything that our culture teaches us about fearing strangers.

The process of creating friends from strangers is one of the most fundamental of human experiences. Just watch children on playgrounds. Jesus talked again and again about how we might find ourselves in need someday, and wouldn't we want the stranger to behave as if they were our neighbor (Luke 10:29-37). Jesus spent his life and ministry touching and being touched by strangers, some of whom loved him, followed him, cared for him, fed him, anointed him, and touched him deeply. Others betrayed or denied, him, beat him and crucified him. Some strangers refused his invitations, including one stranger who the Bible says *Jesus loved.*

I've been attracted to strangers all my life, as have most of us. For various reason, Jesus was attracted to something in this man and called it love. But I also have felt a love for particular strangers, Sometimes when people come to communion at MCC, I have had that experience. People whom I have never seen before, whose names I do not know, come to me for this sacred, intimate spiritual experience, Holy Communion. People come to the communion rail very vulnerable, emotionally and spiritually. They automatically trust that the person who is serving them is trustable, knowing what they are doing, and will not only not harm them, but will minister to them.

What does it mean for me to pray for strangers, to touch them, to feed them, sometimes to hug them, to say their names. And more often than not, I find myself loving them with a love that is more than me. I know it is God's love loving them through me. This is a humbling and wonderful experience, as is having a stranger willing to accept that love from me.

The experience is at once very holy, very tactile, and very demanding. It is a way in which I can provide bodily hospitality to strangers and friends, colleagues and family alike. It is a way in which I sometimes feel a profound solidarity with Jesus and with these strangers as well

And sometimes the strangers themselves are angels. People show up all the time at the church who are probably mentally ill, lost, needy, not even caring what kind of church we are. Some of them are hard to deal with; very few are ever really dangerous. Some of them occasionally bring great gifts of all sorts. I've been prayed for in unbelievable ways by them. Some offer just a smile, or a perspective, or a joke. Sometimes I feel like they are themselves a test for me—especially when they show up on a bad day. Sometimes I feel like they are wasting my time and energy. But when I really think about it, they are not the ones who have really wasted my time and energy.

Isn't the fear of strangers really the basis of racism and homophobia? They are based on fear of those who are different from us in some way. And, if we all start out as strangers, isn't the fear of strangers really the fear of intimacy, of getting close, of being vulnerable? Is this why we have had to find ways to separate sexuality and intimacy? Are we so afraid of our own longings and desires for connection, for closeness, that we have developed a whole culture of fear for strangers? I believe that the unhindered gospel that Jesus embodied calls us to overcome those fears.

Most of our flock came to us as strangers. We have welcomed them with love and acceptance. I remember Rick, a young man with healthy, ruddy skin, prematurely gray hair and bright, twinkling, mischievous eyes. A dreamy, soft-spoken fellow who giggled effeminately, who made dolls and puppets, who wanted to be an artist, who I had first met when he was just 18 or so, in Detroit, Michigan, where I was a young MCC pastor.

Rick and few of his high school friends showed up one night at church upset and weeping. They had driven from "up north" to the big city to find MCC because their best friend had killed himself because he was gay and felt God hated him. On the spur of the moment, responding to their need, our weekly MCC service became a memorial service for their friend. Rick decided that night to move to Detroit and join the church.

Rick was a very handsome, man who loved to clown around. When Rick got AIDS, he was infected with something called psoriatic arthritis, a painful and disfiguring joint disease that also erupted in psoriasis all over his body. When I hadn't seen him at work in a few weeks (he worked across the hall from an office I frequented), I called him at home; I knew he must be very sick.

When I went to see him, his feet were triple their normal size and almost black. He had psoriasis on nearly 75 percent of his body. He could barely hobble to the bathroom and hadn't eaten in days. The psoriasis was in his hair and eyebrows, in what was left of his full beard and mustache, inside his mouth and under his eyelids, inside his ears. In his bed and on the floor were layers of his skin that he had shed. I could have filled a wastebasket with the shed skin. He cried and I cried. I told him he had to go to the hospital. He didn't want to go. I told him if he didn't go voluntarily, I would have to call an ambulance (I wasn't even sure they would take him). I told him if he didn't go, he was going to lose his feet, although I didn't really think they could save them at this point. Finally he agreed to go.

I talked three members of our AIDS ministry team into taking him to the hospital. They carried him down the stairs while he alternately joked and cried. They had to leave all the windows in the car open because the stench was so bad. He was literally rotting from the outside in.

Rick lived almost another six months. They never had to amputate his feet, but neither his feet nor the psoriasis got much better. In the last weeks of his life he could not be touched almost at all because of the excruciating pain and because of the danger to others of the gangrenous infection that covered so much of his body. Yet just before Christmas, Rick was still able to joke and laugh and relate. I will never know how.

Actually, part of Rick's source of grace under pressure was his Mom. When they finally knew their son was terminally ill, Mabel and Amos, Rick's parents, came to help him. Mabel stayed with an MCC church member, George Padilla, and commuted every day to the hospice in Long Beach, quite a long ways away. Amos had had to return home to Michigan to take care of work and other family members.

One day, the cook quit at the hospice, and Mabel just took over the kitchen, moved in, and lived there until Rick's death. In fact, she actually stayed for a few months after he died, because they were so short handed. I was always so grateful for her sacrifice and her attitude of joyful service to everyone at the hospice. They all became her children. In her own way, Mabel's life had taken a "queer turn" as she offered some of the finest in hospitality to "the least of these." Her compassion for her son expanded into a broader, deeper compassion. When I spoke to her about this, she had come to see this sacrifice as a great gift to her in her life, a way of putting Rick's and her own sufferings to some use in the world.

The last time I went to see him, they would not let me in the room, though his mother was able to be with him off and on. The doctors were with him at the time, and it was just too stressful for him to see anyone else. I sat out in the hospice dining room and kept hearing this high pitched scream. It was weeks before I could really allow myself to know that *that sound* had come from Rick. He was so exhausted, his strength so depleted, that he could only cry out in a high-pitched wail that sounded like a child. Now and then, unfortunately, I can still recall it.

He died New Year's Eve 1989, not wanting, I'm sure, to enter another year or decade with such unrelenting pain and suffering. Rick came as a stranger, but left us as one whom was deeply loved.

Ethnic signs and signals are another matter in welcoming strangers. We're not a melting pot, we're more like a tossed salad, retaining the integrity and beauty of each ingredient, not blending and homogenizing them. We have to negotiate frequently about how "user friendly" we are, in a cultural sense, for many kinds of people and cultures. Does everyone who comes to the church recognize something of their own faith and culture in our worship, and does the worship also flow and have coherence and integrity?

We experience this with the Latin ministry at Metropolitan Community Church Los Angeles. Even though many of the participants in our Spanish-language service at one in the afternoon also speak English, it is so comforting and identity-building for many people to worship in an MCC in the Spanish language. It gives the lie to the claim that gays and lesbians are primarily white, Anglo and not Catholic. Also, Latin ministry leaders have struggled to preserve the varied Latin American cultures in our life as a community. For instance, Protestants and Catholics celebrate Holy Week differently and with different intensities. This is compounded by the fact that in many Latin countries, from Holy Thursday at noon through Easter, no one works. It is a prolonged Sabbath. Many Latin people feel very alienated when life goes on as usual during Holy Week in the United States, even if the church has services every evening or all day Sunday.

Also, we had the palms issue. Most Protestants in the U.S. hand out palms on Palm Sunday, and they are pitiful little things, little strips of palm leaves, that Sunday school children would fold into the shape of a cross and pin on their clothing. That, for us, is Palm Sunday.

The first Palm Sunday that the Latin ministry held a service, they were dumbfounded. Palms for Palm Sunday in their experience were huge palm branches that the church members waved as they processed with them into the sanctuary. The next year we had to order two different kinds of palms.

In our church we have two "layers" of tradition. The first is what we bring with us from our ethnic or denominational background. The second layer is the tradition we create. What we want to preserve that which has traditionally brought delight in church experience, especially if it helps visitors feel more at home and welcome at MCC. Some people, still dealing with severe internalized homophobia, wonder if we are a "real" church. They look for signs, some of which are as simple as Does this experience look, sound, smell, feel like church (meaning churches they attended, grew up in)? We have to preach frequently about helping people let go of some of these associations in order to free them from negative aspects of their past religious experience or to make room for others.

Marlene came to MCC Los Angeles one Pentecost Sunday in May. I had met her nearly 18 months before and had been waiting for her to show up. I had spoken at a group on coming out, and she had been a participant. We had connected, and I knew she was filled with religious conflicts. She wanted to come to church but might have a hard time getting there.

It was a gorgeous day, and I was waiting in the small vestibule at Crescent Heights Methodist Church (we were meeting there during the early days of renovation of our church property). I smiled and said, "Good morning, Marlene." She was shocked that I remembered her or her name. But I had remembered. I remembered the intensity, the need. I had prayed for her off and on for quite some time, and I felt that her presence at church as an answer to those prayers. I smiled at her and at the satisfaction of answered prayer.

It was nearly six months before we discovered the importance of Marlene's arrival at MCC on Pentecost. She did not consciously know it was Pentecost. But later on she told me how as a little Portuguese Catholic child, her most precious religious memories were of an annual Portuguese religious festival. There were always parties, wonderful food, and a big parade through the small northern California immigrant town. Each year a little girl was chosen to be the queen of this parade, honoring the Virgin Mary. The festival was a religious and cultural one, in which Marlene took pride. Her fondest memory was of the year she had been chosen to be the queen of the parade, at about age ten. With all the negative and oppressive memories of church and childhood, this festival and her one moment of glory stood out in contrast. It was something precious that she had kept alive in her heart.

Later, she would feel as though that joyful loved feeling she remembered from the festival connected to her experience of God at MCC Los Angeles. She came home to herself in a gay and lesbian church experience that accepted all of who she was—lesbian, Catholic, and Portuguese.

I remember the moment that she was able to tell me that the Portuguese festival was on the feast of Pentecost. I reminded her that her first Sunday at MCC Los Angeles (and her first really adult experience of going to church, at age 40) was also Pentecost. It was as if her mind and body and spirit knew exactly when to return to church. She returned on the very Sabbath day that represented the most affirming, powerful, positive experience of God she had ever had.

This experience, this coincidence was an important part of Marlene's spiritual journey. She had an agenda and a timetable. Marlene had cancer. She came to the church seeking physical and spiritual healing.

A little over two years after that Pentecost, Marlene died of breast cancer. She always expressed her hope for both kinds of healings but rejoiced that she lived long enough to experience a healed, renewed, and joy-filled relationship to God. She learned how to pray, she bought her own Bible and became a virtual "church mouse," present nearly every time the doors were open. And when she felt well enough to come. She basked in the freedom to think and feel and pray to the God of her own heart and under standing, like a child welcomed home after a glorious parade. The memory of her still blesses us at Pentecost and throughout the year.

# Conclusion—A Queer Millennium?

Bishop William Boyd Grove, chair of yet another NCC/UFMCC dialogue effort (and more recently, the trial judge at the trial of Methodist minister Jimmy Creech), said in one of our committee meetings that he thinks that homosexuality as an issue is like the little thread dangling from the lining of his coat. It doesn't look like such a big deal by itself, but he hears his wife saying, "Whatever you do, don't pull that thread!" Because if he does, the whole lining of his coat will fall out! Church leaders instinctively know perhaps that the issue of homosexuality is only the most visible issue in a connected fabric of issues about human sexuality that the Church cannot bear to see unravel.

Meanwhile, gays and lesbians continue to be vilified in our culture on the basis of outdated and thoroughly disputed homophobic interpretations of a few mostly obscure passages of Scripture. We at UFMCC do not have the power on our own to overturn this situation, at least not easily and not as quickly as it needs to happen. The leaders of the churches in the United States and around the world must take responsibility for what they know.

At one point in our stormy relationship, I teased the National Council of Churches of Christ in the U.S.A. I said, "Do you know where I see the greatest unhappiness about sexuality in the world today? Not in the gay and lesbian community. Not in the prisons or hospitals I visit. Not even in the streets. The greatest unhappiness about sexuality I see is at meetings of the National Council of Churches." And by that I meant that sometimes I felt as if MCC should have a counseling room at the meetings. Often we did, but it was my hotel room or the hotel rooms of other UFMCC visitors at the NCC.

Sometimes we counseled in hallways or doorways. People would seek us out to talk about their gay son or daughter, their child with AIDS, men who were gay but couldn't tell their wives. A heterosexually married staff person's lover died of AIDS, but he could tell no one. He sobbed in my arms in the corner of a meeting room. Men and women whose marriages were troubled for other reasons would choose us to talk to. I held governing board members in my arms who cried about their divorces or the struggles of being widowed. Some harbored shameful secrets or sought us out with painful questions. Some came to me wanting to know if I thought that so-and-so was gay.

Others knocked on our doors late at night hoping to God no one saw them. Some people would never be caught dead talking to me, not realizing that that in itself was a dead giveaway.

I could always tell who the gay or lesbian or bisexual people were at a conference with the "pamphlet test." We would put out our pamphlets on a table with other literature. People would glance at them, some would pick them up to peruse them, some would take copies. But if the person saw our literature and then looked furtively over his or her shoulder ("Were any religious police lurking nearby?") before putting it down or taking it, I knew he or she was struggling with shame or guilt, I knew he or she was probably gay or lesbian.

Some people were cruel and judgmental and asked inappropriate and prying questions they would never ask of a heterosexual person or wish to be asked themselves. There were people who knocked on our doors late at night looking for sex. Others who came on to us at the dinner table, or under the dinner table, or sitting next to us on a bus on the way to an NCC event. Men who thought lesbian meant "hard to get" or that it meant we were bisexual or liked "three-ways" or that we were open to "kinky" sex. We who were supposed to be worldly and sophisticated about such matters found ourselves shocked at times, amused and sometimes not amused.

Some folks would proposition us for sex and then vote against us on the floor of National Council of Churches of Christ meetings. They were self-hating homosexuals, bisexuals or heterosexuals experimenting while away from home. Sometimes the temptation to "out" these folks was nearly more than we could bear.

In November of 1992, in Cleveland, Ohio, at the General Board meeting, the NCC voted narrowly not to accept UFMCC as an observer to the

NCC. (We were already observers to the WCC.) At the time, even non-Christian organizations were so designated by the Council: the Unitarians (which include Christians, but do not have a trinitarian Christian doctrine), a Muslim group and a Jewish organization all were observers of the NCC. There was in fact no criteria for observer status. We actually applied to be observers as a semi-graceful way of ending a long and painful (disgraceful at times) "dialogue to nowhere" that ended up being just a prolonged stalling tactic for not dealing with our membership application. We simply had no idea that asking to end all the silliness by settling for observer status would be controversial. But they debated for five hours about it, and voted no.

No officer of the NCC spoke in our favor, or even volunteered to clarify the issue. From the floor, Dr. Paul Sherry, head of the United Church of Christ, along with the Methodists and a few others, pleaded for rationality. But to no avail. One young lesbian, a visitor (not from UFMCC) said, quite sincerely, "Even if you (the NCC) thought UFMCC was of the devil, wouldn't you want them to observe you so they could learn how real Christians act?"

It has been my privilege and joy to work with "real Christians," and people of real and courageous faith, Christian or not. Telling these stories has made me hopeful: that new generations of "our tribe(s)" will take up the banner of justice and inclusion, in and outside of the Church. Everyday someone comes out of a closet. Everyday, someone is born who will one day come out as gay, lesbian, bisexual or transgendered. What kind of world will they inherit? What new opportunities will they have? What new visions will they create and implement?

As the new millennium begins, we continue our work in faith and truth and in pride of our sure knowledge of Christ's teachings of love, service and forgiveness. And we never forget his promise of hope.

I imagine a time to come when MCC along with gay men and lesbian in all churches will be welcomed with outstretched arms, a time when we wait at the gathering of the world's religions with our banner to remind them that "God loves all people," and it's a banner we never need to unfurl. I imagine a time when the Church becomes a true reflection of Christ's inclusive teachings. What a powerful thought! This is still a queer millennial vision. But hold on, *our time is coming.*

Rev. Nancy Wilson

# Notes

### Introduction—Tribal Tales

1. Metropolitan Community Church is a denomination founded in 1968 by Rev. Troy Perry with a special outreach to lesbians, gay men and bisexuals but open to all people. For the story of MCC, read Rev. Troy Perry, *The Lord is My Shepherd and He Knows I'm Gay* (Los Angeles; UFMCC Press, 1994) and Perry, *Don' t Be Afraid Anymore* (NewYork: St. Martin's Press, 1990). See also Frank S. Mead, *The Handbook of Denominations,* new 9th ed. revised by Samuel Hill (Nashville, TN: Abingdon Press, 1990), p. 167.

2. Judy Grahn, *Another Mother Tongue* (Boston: Beacon Press, 1984), p. 6.

3. See Michael Cartwright, "Ideology and Interpretation of the Bible in the African-American Tradition," *Modern Theology* (April 1993).

4. The National Council of Churches, headquartered at 475 Riverside Drive, New York, was founded in 1950 and is the successor to the defunct Federal Council of Churches. In its heyday, it founded Church World Services, had a social activisit reputation and was a fairly progressive vanguard of the mainline churches in America, helping to fund, for example Martin Luther King, Jr.'s march on Washington in 1963.

5. Martin Buber, *I and Thou* (NewYork: Scribners, 1970) p. 108.

6. Originally the word was not *martyrs* but *heretics,* according to Rev. Jim Mitulski, pastor of MCC San Francisco.

7. Juston Gonzales, *Out of Every Tribe and Nation: Christian Theology at the Ethical Roundtable* (Nashville: Abingdon Press, 1992).

8. Ibid., p. 26.

9. Ibid., p. 33

10. See Susan Thistlewaite, *Sex, Race, and God: Christian Feminism in Black and White* (New York: Crossroads, 1991).

11. Perry, the Lord Is My Shepherd, P. 201.

12. The same story is told in "An Improbably Pair," *Lotus of Another Color* (Boston: Alyson Publications, 1993). pp. 175-189.

13. Transcription of Chris Cowap's remarks to the NCC governing borad, November 9, 1983 in Hartford.

14. The Lima Liturgy was proposed by the WCC Commission on Faith and Order and was composed at a conference in Lima, Peru, prior to the 1991 General Assembly. It is the first ecumenical liturgy composed and celebrated by such a diverse international Christian body.

## Chapter One—Healing Our Tribal Wounds

1. Emily Dickinson, "I Never Saw a Moor" *The Poems of Emily Dickinson,* Thomas H. Johnson, et al (Cambridge, MA: Belknap Press of Harvard University Press, 1955).

2. Angela Davis, "Rape, Racism, and the Myth of the Black Rapist," in *Women, Race, and Class* (New York: Random House, 1981), pp. 172-201.

3. *Presbyterians and Human Sexuality* (Louisville, KY: Office of the General Assembly, Lousiville, KY, 1991), p. 2.

## Chapter Two—Boldly Exercizing Our Tribal Gifts

1. M. Scott Peck, *People of the Lie* (New York: Simon and Schuster, 1983).

2. Harry Hay, "A Separate People Whose Time Has Come," in Mark Thompson, ed. *Gay Spirit* (New York: St. Martin's Press, 1987), pp. 279-291.

3. Freda Smith, "Dear Dora/Dangerous Deek Diesel Dyke," used with permission of the author.

4. Carter Heywood, *Touching Our Strength: The Erotic as Power and the Love of God* (San Francisco: Harper and Row, 1989).

5. Nelle Morton, *The Journey Is Home* (Boston: Beacon Press, 1985), chap. 1, 23.

6. Lucia Chappelle, "Silent Night, Raging Night," in *DeColores MCC Hymnal* (Los Angeles: 1983), p. 6.

7. Mark Thompson, "Children of Paradise: A Brief History of Queens," in Thompson, *Gay Spirit,* p. 52.

8. Hay "A Separate People," p. 285.

9. Ibid., p. 280.

10. Edmund Begler, *Homosexuality, Disease or Way of Life?* (New York: Hill and Wang, 1956).

11. Rosemary Radford Ruether, *Sexism and God Talk* (Boston: Beacon Press, 1983), pp. 82, 170-172.

## Chapter Three—A New Lens on the Bible.

1. Robert Goss, *Jesus Acted Up* (San Francisco: HarperSan Francisco, 1993).

2. Phyllis Trible, *Texts of Terror* (Philadelphia: Fortress Press, 1984). Phyllis Trible first used this phrase to denote Bible passages that described or justified violence toward women.

3. The "texts of terror" for gay and lesbian Christians are Genesis 19, Leviticus 18:22 and 20:13, Romans 1:26-27, Corinthians 6:9 and 1Timothy 1:10.

4. Daniel Helminiak, *What the Bible Really Says About Homosexuality* (San Francisco: Alamo Square Press, 1994).

5. See Tex Sample, *Hard-Living People and Mainstream Christians,* (Nashville, TN: Abingdon Press, 1993) for his definition and description of the sociology and spirituality of "hard-living people."

## Chapter Four—Equal to Angels

1. Jean Foye, "Reluctant Prophet," from her collection of unpublished poems that she left to the author.

2. Foye, "But Not Forgotten," from her collection of unpublished poems.

# Other Books of the Spirit from Alamo Square Press

## Being • Being Happy • Being Gay

Pathways to a Rewarding Life for Lesbians and Gay Men. The make-your-life-work book by Bert Herrman. "Herrman extends a compassionate and useful hand in the journey toward realizing our full human potential." —Mark Thompson, *The Advocate*. ISBN: 0-9624751-0-6/paper/$8.00

## In God's Image

Christian Witness to the Need for Gay/Lesbian Equality in the Eyes of the Church by (Episcopal) Fr. Robert Warren Cromey. "Nurturing, healing...a call to action."—Malcolm Boyd. ISBN: 0-9624751-2-2/paper/$9.95

## Out of the Bishop's Closet

The Daring Testimony of Faith of a Gay Mormon High Priest by Antonio A. Feliz. Fleeing the tyranny of the Church, Feliz escapes with secrets that would make Brigham Young turn pale. ISBN: 0-9624751-7-3/paper/$12.95

## Out with a Passion

A United Methodist Pastor's Quest for Authenticity by Dr. Richard T. Rossiter. Rich Rossiter had it all: He was pastor of a thriving church. He had a devoted wife and two wonderful children. However, something was wrong. This is Rossiter's journal and dialogue with God as he faced the difficult path to truth. ISBN: 1-886360-07-3/paper/$11.95.

## What the Bible *Really* Says About Homosexuality
### (Millennium Edition)

Recent findings by top scholars offer a radical new view. The long-awaited, mind-expanding bestseller by Daniel A. Helminiak, Ph.D., a Roman Catholic Priest and respected theologian. *Now expanded and updated.* 1-886360-09-X/paper/$14.00.

To purchase copies of these books, send a check or money order for the price of each book requested plus $2.00 for the first book and $.50 for each additional book (for postage and handling) to:

Alamo Square Distributors
P.O. Box 2510
Novato, CA 94948

Checks must be drawn in U.S. currency. There is no additional cost for shipping to Canada, but readers from all other countries are required to send send $5.00 per book (for air-mail postage and handling).